Please
Don't
Kill
the
Mockingbirds

*a story of forgiveness
and redemption*

MARY ANN SANDERS

This book is lovingly dedicated to one of the sweetest, most gentle, and genuinely kind servants I have ever known, the late Katherine T. Fabin. She served faithfully as housemother at Shepherd's Arms Ministry for thirteen years.

Katie tried to teach me about humility by the life she lived before me every day. She tried to teach me how to best protect the little mockingbirds we served, and she inspired me to want to kiss Narcissus good-bye. Katie, I'm still working on it.

TABLE OF CONTENTS

PREFACE

Question: What is the chief end of man?

Answer: To glorify God and enjoy Him forever.[1]

Please Don't Kill the Mockingbirds is a testimonial to the extraordinary power of the resurrected Lord in the life of an ordinary woman. It is living proof that God Almighty can transform the deepest human pain into His magnificent glory.

This book is a reflection of a journey of salvific new birth in which a victim of abuse and narcissism is moved resiliently to a posture of victor and servant of God. It retraces the miraculous fingerprints of Jesus in a life that has chosen to leave the confines of pride, hatred, shame, bitterness, rage, and unforgiveness in order to join Him in the redemptive and reconciling work He is doing in His kingdom. This is a work aimed at glorifying God while enjoying His presence and encouraging others to do the same.

The purpose of this book is to offer hope to the hopeless, courage to the fearful, joy to the grieving, peace to the conflicted, vitality to the depressed, and faith to the faithless. The methodology for healing the wounded and broken demonstrated in this work is found in one word—*forgiveness*. Receiving and giving the forgiveness of God first to one's self and then freely passing it on to others from the heart is the construct for this work.

Woven into the fabric of this piece is a transcript of how a ministry was birthed and sustained for a quarter of a century and continues on today. It is a study in faith that emerges out of the ashes of defeat, despondency, and discouragement. *Please Don't Kill the Mockingbirds* is a literal transcript of how the Lord protects the innocent and very weakest fledglings and gives them supernatural strength to take flight with scarred wings and soar like eagles.

As you begin to read this book, I pray this prayer for you:

So I kneel humbly in awe before the Father of our Lord Jesus, the Messiah, the perfect Father of every father and child in heaven and on the earth. And I pray that he would unveil within you the unlimited riches of his glory and favor until supernatural strength floods your innermost being with his divine might and explosive power.

Then, by constantly using your faith, the life of Christ will be released deep inside you, and the resting place of his love will become the very source and root of your life.

Then you will be empowered to discover what every holy one experiences—the great magnitude of the astonishing love of Christ in all its dimensions. How deeply intimate and far-reaching is his love! How enduring and inclusive it is! Endless love beyond measurement that transcends our understanding—this extravagant love pours into you until you are filled to overflowing with the fullness of God!

— EPHESIANS 3:14–19 TPT

Chapter 1

IN THE BEGINNING
THERE WAS PAIN

*For I consider that the sufferings of
this present time are not worthy to be
compared with the glory which shall be
revealed in us.*

— ROMANS 8:18

Old Heaven Hill whiskey number 80 proof was
stacked in his closet by the case, and our
refrigerator was packed to the brim with Schlitz
beer. I don't know if Schlitz is actually the beer
that made Milwaukee famous, but it sure left an
ugly, indelible scar on our family. Old Heaven Hill
was a misnomer too because it brought nothing
but hell to our little hill in North Chattanooga.
One time I got so fed up with Old Heaven Hill
that I opened every single bottle and poured

Morton Salt into them. Boy howdy, did that start World War III! I almost didn't make it out of that war zone alive.

Those old movies playing in my mind remind me of one of my most favorite books that started off with the protagonist confessing, "When I was little, I would think of ways to kill my daddy. I would figure it out this way or that and would run it down through my head until it got easy."[2] Author Kaye Gibbons couldn't have phrased my personal prayers any better. When I was a little girl, I would beg God if He was really real to please take my daddy away from us so he couldn't abuse us anymore. My daddy was a veteran of World War II. He came home from the war with something my grandmama called being shell-shocked. From shell shock he quickly graduated and became a raging alcoholic and philanderer. Way back in 1956 we didn't know about post-traumatic stress disorder, but I learned about it firsthand and believe me, it is transferrable. It's much more contagious than any computer virus.

---

2   Kaye Gibbons, *Ellen Foster* (New York: Knopf Doubleday Publishing Group, 1997), 1.

I was an only child and still vividly remember when my daddy would come home at three in the morning so drunk that he was out of his mind. He would run through the house yelling and tearing pictures off the walls, wanting to pick a fight with someone. Guess I was the only thing standing between my mama and his fist. The real truth was—I dearly loved my daddy, and so did my mama. We couldn't understand why he didn't know that. Most of all we couldn't figure out why he wanted to hurt us when he was drinking. Why would you marry someone, have a child, and then try to hurt them? Maybe Matlock or Perry Mason could have solved this case more quickly, but it took me thirty long years to close out the mystery. The answer to this convoluted story is simply that wounded people wound people.

It was easy to see why my daddy married my mama—she was literally a beauty queen. She held the title of Miss Cleveland in her youth and had all the looks to back it up. Her sparkling, deep baby blue eyes provided the perfect backdrop for her flowing natural blond hair, perfectly applied makeup, and stylish gray suede high-heel pumps that matched her soft, light-colored gray cashmere sweater dress. She always groomed herself this way for a day in the office at Buster Brown Hosiery Mill. She was sleek and slim, and as Jonathan Swift would say, "She was a good sight for sore eyes." No one would ever suspect my mama had been up all night fighting for her life and mine with a fragmented war veteran.

When the five o'clock whistle would blow at the hosiery mill, my mama would pick up her gray suede briefcase, get into her 1955 blue-and-white Chevy Belair, and head out for her second-shift job selling real estate. She was a whiz of a sales lady and sold real estate as though her life depended on it. When she retired from Buster Brown several years later, she opened her own real estate company, and the company prospered for more than fifty years.

Although I was only eight years old, I stood up tall and brave for my mama. This task was daunting. We rarely ate a meal that my daddy didn't throw his plate of gravy and biscuits across the room just perfectly to make the gravy ooze slowly down the walls. Once I watched while he broke my mama's finger from twisting it repetitively like a corkscrew in a bottle of wine. Another time he smashed a drinking glass and cut my mama's arm until she bled like Old Faithful just because he didn't like the supper menu. Even though that was sixty years ago, those graphic flashback movies still occasionally pop up in my mind uninvited.

Every now and again something funny would wedge itself between agony and anguish and give us a little pleasurable relief. One example is the time my mama scrambled some eggs and mixed them with canned dog food in our dog Cocoa's bowl. Mama took a quick bathroom break and left the scrambled egg mixture on the counter. Cocoa wasn't feeling well, and Mama fully intended to feed the mixture to him. My daddy came home unexpectedly. He ate up that dog food in one big gulp and asked my mama for more. My mama and I couldn't quit laughing—secretly, of course.

Year after year after year of dysfunction piled up like a hoarder piles up old, dingy newspapers. Before I realized it, I was a senior in high school. My greatest high-school fear was to have a date on Friday night and my daddy show up and park his bent-up, already sideways car in the middle of the street and stagger into the house as we were leaving. I wish I had a silver dollar for every time that happened because I would have had a handsome scholarship fund for college.

Finally, I did go away to the University of Tennessee in Knoxville. Now my great big worry was my daddy just might beat my mama to death when he was in a drunken stupor. After one year of escalated abuse and constant worry and anxiety about my mama, I decided to move back home to Chattanooga so I could help defend her. After all, I always thought my daddy and mama's issues were my fault.

My mama would never discuss the abuse with anyone and would deny accusations that my daddy was an alcoholic or unfaithful in any way. But one night my daddy came home totally out of control and tried to harm my mother in unspeakable ways. I stepped in to try to defend her, and he threw me into the floor and tried to choke me to death. Thankfully my mama climbed out a window and called a friend for help. My mama also called our home telephone number and the ringing phone shocked my father enough that he stopped choking me and I was able to escape.

After that episode my mama took me away to an apartment to live where we could be safe, where we thought my daddy couldn't hurt us physically or emotionally anymore. Little did we know the lingering traumatizing effects of that kind of dysfunction goes on year after year after year. My mama lived in a constant state of anxiety, fear, and high blood pressure even though the source of danger was no longer present. All those years of my daddy's alcoholic abuse and running around with other women had set up like concrete in her soul. Even though I was only nineteen years old, I was also feeling irrational fears as I attended a local university and worked second shift as a telephone operator. I guess I had a mild case of PTSD after spending so many consecutive years on the nocturnal battlefield.

Late one morning someone knocked violently on our apartment door. I opened the door and saw my cousin Kenneth, who blurted out some of the most paralyzing words of my life. Kenneth was breathless as he said, "We found your daddy dead on the kitchen floor at Mama Mallie's. He still had the cigarette he was trying to light between his fingers, and rigor mortis had already set in." At nineteen years old my world stopped on its axis, crashed and burned in less than five seconds. I wasn't a Christian but somehow God had answered my foolish and selfish childhood prayer ten years later.

The last time I had seen my father alive was three weeks prior to his death as I walked through my Mama Mallie's kitchen and ignored him as he spoke to me. Why was I so angry? Why so bitter? Several weeks before he died, I was driving across the Walnut Street Bridge in my convertible and saw him kissing what the Bible defines as "a strange woman." I later found out that this strange woman was a meter maid. Unbeknownst to her, she had parked her car in the wrong garage this time. I wheeled my little red MGB around and drove right up onto the sidewalk, where I planned to run them over and be done with it. Fortunately, they escaped my wrath.

Now just a few weeks later he was really dead at the age of forty-seven, and I hadn't been speaking to him at the time of his death. No more abuse, no more abandonment, no more Old Heaven Hill or Schlitz, no more gravy oozing down the walls, and no more Daddy Jim. Gone like the wind, just like that. He was finally gone, but he had left an eighteen-wheeler truckload of emotional baggage behind for us to unpack and rearrange. Sometimes we get what we ask for even when we really didn't mean for God to answer our prayers that way.

Grief work is the hardest work on earth, and you can't contract it out because nobody can do it for you. As we prepared for the funeral, we were all smitten with guilt, shame, condemnation, and wall-to-wall regret. The day of the visitation we received an unexpected and unwelcomed phone call from a woman who said she was married to my daddy. The problem with that was my mama was still married to my daddy. It seems he had gotten rip-roaring drunk and married this strange woman, forgetting to tell her the detail that he was already married. And now this strange woman planned to crash his funeral service. I told her that if she showed up we would make it a double-header. It was five years before I met Jesus Christ as my Lord, so I was acting perfectly normal for my current spiritual status. Sinners always act like sinners. This strange woman was attempting to add insult to injury. After our heart-to-heart conversation, she decided it was safer to stay home to grieve my daddy's passing privately.

Chapter 2

MY SWEET IRISH SAINT

. . . strengthened with all might, according to His glorious power, for all patience and long-suffering with joy; giving thanks to the Father who has qualified us to be partakers of the inheritance of the saints in the light.

—COLOSSIANS 1:11–12

Before we go any further, I need to tell you about my Mama Mallie. She was my daddy's mama. I had stayed with her during the day from the time I was four years old until I left for college. She lived four blocks from Buster Brown Hosiery Mill, where my mama worked. My mama had to go to work to support our family since my daddy had a full-time job supporting Old Heaven Hill and Schlitz brewing companies. After all, somebody had to buy the gravy and biscuits he used to baptize our kitchen walls.

My Mama Mallie was a saint. She taught the old ladies' Sunday school class down at the Baptist church for many years. When she and my mama would dress up for church, you just better strike up the band because they looked better than the Easter parade. Honey, I mean they had hats, gloves, shoes, and dresses that matched perfectly. Now my Mama Mallie weighed at least three hundred fifty pounds and spent all her time in the kitchen cooking for everyone in her family and the church. I can still picture her in a simple homemade cotton print dress with an apron tied around her waist, ornate pink plastic glasses riding low on her nose, sweat-filled brow, and always a little out of breath as she shuffled around her kitchen floor in black felt house shoes that came from the five-and-dime. It was the very same kitchen floor where my daddy died.

All day long she kept the radio playing sermons or some kind of spiritual encouragement as a backdrop for her home missions ministry. My goodness gracious, she could fry up some chicken legs even better than the Colonel himself. Every Friday come rain or shine we would head out to the Piggy Wiggly supermarket in East Brainerd that my Aunt Ann and Uncle Prince owned so we could stock up with those chicken legs. I still dream about her zebra pudding made with chocolate wafers layered between thick whipped cream. Those chocolate wafers could be bought only at Kay's Castle, where the ice cream was to die for. The zebra pudding had to be put into the refrigerator all night so the whipped cream could ooze and soak perfectly into every morsel and crumb of those chocolate wafers. Mama Mallie always kept a huge pot of Standard Coffee brewing in the kitchen. Back then, the Standard Coffee truck would deliver bags of coffee right to your doorstep.

Those days were filled with all kinds of wonderful home deliveries including those of the ice-cream man with one wooden peg leg who pushed his little cart through the neighborhood and rang a cow bell to announce his arrival. My dog Pat, a sweet jet-black Scottie, and I had a standing credit account with him. Every day we shared a huge ten-cent cup of vanilla. I took a lick, then Pat took his turn. We never needed those wooden sticks because our cream never lasted long enough to use them. Then there was the hot tamale man with his little pushcart, the Fuller Brush man—and my favorite, Dr. Buttram, our family doctor. I had his footsteps memorized as he would walk across Mama Mallie's front porch. He was a regular visitor since my Granddaddy Elmer had both legs amputated and required many therapeutic visits.

I had a secret daytime combat zone going on with one delivery man who drove a bread truck. He showed up in a great big truck with wide-opened side doors, so every rock I hurled at him would be spot on. I would hide behind my grandmother's big hickory nut tree and let those rocks fly hard and fast just as he exited the big tunnel coming through Missionary Ridge onto Tinker Street. He always stopped to tattle on me to Mama Mallie. She was my greatest advocate, and she firmly told him her baby would never do anything like that. I would just put on my angelic face and smile and agree with her as I surreptitiously pushed the extra rocks down deeper in my pockets. All those rocks must have been a way to ventilate and express all the deep, sweltering anger I had repressed by the grand old age of seven.

My great uncles, especially the ones with diabetes, would stop by every day to have a dunking party with me—vanilla wafers and Standard Coffee. That's the way I survived the nightly war zone at my own house—I attended a daily healing tent in Mama Mallie's kitchen. I guess you may have figured out by now that she was Irish and her maiden name was O'Neal. Mama Mallie rescued every hobo, drunk, and abused child she found. Sometimes when I would arrive in the morning, the hobos would be lined up on her back steps waiting for her to feed them. Before I ever entered her door, I could smell the coffee brewing and the chicken frying. Her prayers are what saved me physically and spiritually. As a child I felt I could look straight into the depths of her heart and see Jesus staring right square back at me.

I finally figured out just how much my Mama Mallie loved me when I was a sophomore in high school and needed a ride to school. She had not driven a car in twenty years, but she bought one of those Nash Ambassador Ramblers with push buttons so she could drive me to school. I think she believed those push buttons were supposed to be easy buttons that substituted for driving skills. I often wished for a push-button escape hatch.

When she rolled into the driver's seat, she was so short that she could barely see over the steering wheel. That turquoise-and-white push-button car should have come with a safety helmet for the passengers, but it didn't. When she drove me to school at five miles an hour, I would duck and hide when I saw my classmates. I always made her let me out several blocks away from Central High School. It must have taken great faith for her to drive after all those years, and I know it took more than great faith to ride with her.

My sweet Mama Mallie died with a brain tumor, the doctors said. I will add she had a broken heart from my daddy's untimely death. I remember sitting alone with her all night for thirty nights at the hospital and watching as she had grand mal seizures. While sitting with her, I spent a lot of time reflecting on my childhood and all the love she had lavishly poured out on me. When the Lord came to get her to take her to heaven one morning at five o'clock, I was all alone with her. She was the first person I had ever seen die but certainly not the last. My Mama Mallie had been the mama I spent most of every day of my life with from the time I was four years old until age eighteen, when I left for college. She had been my spiritual umbilical cord that connected me to Jesus until the time of my spiritual birth, when I was twenty-five.

Chapter 3

GOOD UNDERSTANDING PRODUCES FAVOR

Good understanding gains favor, But the way of the unfaithful is hard.

— PROVERBS 13:15

By this time I suppose you are thinking I really hated my daddy. Not true. In fact, nothing could be further from the truth. I always loved my daddy and still do today, but I never cared for his behavior when he was drinking alcohol. My daddy was a genius, a genuine brainiac. My daddy and his daddy were both amazingly gifted building contractors. They would build subdivision after subdivision of houses designed by my daddy. When he was sober he would sit up all night and draw elaborate, detailed house plans for an entire subdivision and then go out and build it. He also loved music and gave me an appreciation for the fine arts at a very young age. One of my most precious memories was listening to him sing "The Lord's Prayer" when he was shaving. Twenty years after he died, the Lord reminded me of my daddy's love for Him even though he was a shattered, torn-apart World War II veteran.

In my mind's eye I can still see my daddy sitting around my Mama Mallie's dining table in his cuffed khaki pants, starched and ironed long-sleeved white shirt with sleeves rolled halfway up above his elbows, and oxblood penny loafers with argyle socks. His jet-black hair with graying temples was framed by a huge cloud of smoke rising from his unfiltered Camel cigarette as he drank black Standard Coffee and worked massive crossword puzzles like the ones in the Sunday paper. When he dressed up to go out drinking, he would always wear a snazzy burgundy-shaded bow tie with cute bright-white polka dots and a dashing streamlined navy blue dress suit. My daddy was a very striking and extremely handsome man. By the time he arrived back home between three and four in the morning, his bow tie was hanging sideways and limp, and his suit was all ruffled and exhausted.

When my Daddy Jim was sober, he was more fun to be around than ten barrels of monkeys. He would sit for hours and play dominoes with me and let me win. When it snowed he would take me riding in his old sideways car, and we would drive up the steepest part of Missionary Ridge without snow tires or chains just to see if we could. On rainy days he would always help me with my book reports. He would read the book and then do the report for me. He was very creative and made up the best homemade jokes. My favorite one was when he would drive by the Jewish temple on McCallie Avenue and ask, "Do you know what kind of lights they have in there?" Since he was a builder everyone thought he really knew about the lighting in the temple. They would say, "No, Jim—what kind of lights?" His answer was given with a cute little laugh as he said, "Israelites, of course!" If my Daddy Jim could have divorced Old Heaven Hill and Schlitz beer, our lives would have been drastically different.

Proverbs 13:15 says good understanding produces favor. Let me tell you how very true that statement is. Acquisition of good understanding of the casualties of World War II enhanced exponentially my depth of love and respect for my Daddy Jim. Reflecting over the past, I have discovered underneath the foul smell of Old Heaven Hill and Schlitz Beer was a desperate scent of despondency, anxiety, helplessness, dark depression, and vast woundedness that longed to be held securely in the arms of love, understanding, and acceptance. He hungered for answers and empathy and a quiet acceptance of who he was and what he had suffered. The real words projected from his silent lips every time he took a swig of Old Heaven Hill were *help me, help me, somebody please help me numb this pain.*

My daddy was a faithful member of the "Greatest Generation" Tom Brokaw wrote about.[3] He was a war hero who enlisted because it was the right thing to do. Being the tough guys they were, the Greatest Generation practiced faithfully holding all their emotions inside rather than dumping them onto their families. Even though World War II had ended August 14, 1945, my daddy's war had just begun and continued on

---

3   Tom Brokaw, *The Greatest Generation* (New York: Random House, 1998).

until the day he died. Now my daddy was no longer fighting Germany, Japan, or Italy but his war theater included the night terrors, survivor's guilt, exaggerated startle responses, heavy drinking, and profound and lingering sadness caused by the demonic memories that plagued his mind day and night with no rest, no vacation, no time-out to find a respite.

He was almost killed in the Battle of the Bulge when a shell ricocheted off his helmet, traumatizing him. He encountered another miraculous incident when a bullet hit the metal-encased pocket-sized New Testament he carried over his heart in his uniform. Both of these incidents saved his physical life but waged war on his mental, emotional, social, and spiritual life. Those free mental World War II movies that played around the clock at such a devastatingly high price afforded my daddy constant agony and misery. The soldiers in World War II saw more blood and guts spilled and fleshly carnage of death, disfigurement, and horrors than any human being should be permitted to witness. It's no wonder a large majority of the returning war heroes felt isolated and crazy, thinking it was all just because they were weak. In 2015 an article in *The Washington Post*[4] spoke of the skeptics of shell shock or other combat-related neuroses. The article cites General George Patten, who slapped two hospitalized soldiers in 1943 who were being treated for what is now labeled post-traumatic stress disorder (PTSD), calling one a "yellow bastard." Thankfully, Patton was sternly reprimanded by Allied Commander General Dwight Eisenhower. The article went on to give some very interesting stats about these World War II veterans. "In World War II some 16 million Americans served in the armed forces with fewer than half seeing actual combat. Of those who saw actual combat more than 1 million were discharged for combat-related neuroses, according to military stats. Interestingly enough in 1947 nearly half the beds in every VA hospital in the nation were still occupied by soldiers with no visible wounds."

Those invasive invisible wounds were devastating to my daddy and to our family. I suppose the question must be asked, "Can a child of a fragmented World War II veteran take a lickin'

---

4   Tim Madigan, "Their War Ended 70 Years Ago, Their Trauma Didn't," *The Washington Post* (September 11, 2015).

and keep on tickin'?" The ultimate answer will be given in the pages that follow.

My daddy was my hero even though it's taken a lifetime of pain to uncover that marvelous truth. My daddy's faithful service to his beloved country makes me so very proud of him and proud to be an American! Most importantly, now I can honestly say I am blessed to be called my Daddy Jim's daughter!

Chapter 4

PAIN TRANSFORMED
INTO GAIN

For His anger is but for a moment, His
favor is for life; Weeping may endure for a
night, but joy comes in the morning."

— PSALM 30:5

My daddy's funeral service was numbing for me emotionally. Funeral services are devastating for unbelievers and children plagued with unforgiveness, bitterness, and rage. The days and months went by slowly, and the emotional suffering lingered and grew like a tick on a hound dog for the next fifteen years, but somehow I finally finished college with a Bachelor of Science Degree in Music after eight years and five or six different majors.

In the months after we buried my daddy, I experienced wall-to-wall grief as my Mama Mallie died the very next year, followed by my beloved piano instructor of fifteen years. Music with emphasis on piano performance had been a major part of my life since I was five years old. I had studied at Cadek Conservatory of Music with the same instructor from age five until I was a senior in college when my instructor died from breast cancer at a very young age. I was lost, confused, bewildered, and depressed after this series of deaths. Unforgiveness, bitterness, and rage wrapped around me like a boa constrictor, slowly squeezing the life out of my soul day by day. Even though this is an oxymoron, I was secretly angry at God. The truth was, my anger and hatred were of myself. I still blamed myself for my parents' issues and for my daddy's untimely death.

I had some faithful friends at the university who realized my life was torn and fragmented into a zillion pieces. These friends loved me enough to invite me to a place called Reach Out Ranch, better known today as Precept Ministries. Kay Arthur taught the Word of God line upon line and precept upon precept. I signed up for an inductive Bible study course on the Gospel of

John at Reach Out Ranch. That was about forty-five years ago, when the meetings were still held in an old barn. The very first time I went there, I heard a young man sing "Jesus, Jesus, Jesus! There's just something about that name."[5] That song connected with something deep inside my soul and made me want to find out more about this Jesus.

The message Kay Arthur delivered from the Word of God also stirred up a hunger and thirst for righteousness. What was I missing? My soul was empty and longing for something more than life had given me up to this point.

The Lord was working overtime in my life because simultaneously our banker, who was also a choir director, invited me to play the piano at a local Baptist church. One Sunday evening after playing the piano for a church service and hearing an anointed sermon, I felt the conviction of the Holy Spirit drawing me into the kingdom of God. It was nine at night and the formal church service was over, but I remembered my pastor often ate at Sambo's Restaurant. I got into my car and drove

---

5   Bill and Gloria Gaither, "There's Something About That Name," © 1970 William J. Gaither.

over to Sambo's on Brainerd Road, where I told my pastor that I had to have Jesus in my heart right away. He immediately got up from his meal, and we went back to his church office, where he counseled me. I prayed the sinner's prayer and was born again of the Holy Spirit.

I was twenty-five years old when I became a Christian. At that point in my life I was not a tough old bird but a very vulnerable young fledging in Christ. However, I could feel my song being slowly transformed from a requiem to a melodic rhapsody. Yes, I became a new creation in Christ, and yes, I was born again, but that subtle boa constrictor of unforgiveness, bitterness, and rage remained wrapped tightly around my soul for the next fifteen years. Narcissism had built massive strongholds in my mind, will, and emotions that needed to be removed. There was another blockade preventing freedom from emerging—the perspective I held of myself as a victim. Victims, I have discovered, can be their own worst enemies.

Chapter 5

ANSWERING
THE CALL

But you shall receive power when the Holy Spirit has come upon you; and you shall be witnesses to Me in Jerusalem, and in all Judea and Samaria, and to the end of the earth.

— ACTS 1:8

At this juncture in my life I felt like the monk who signed up for service in a silent monastery and took the vow of silence where you could say only two words once a year. After the first year had passed, when the Monsignor asked the young monk what he had to say about the monastery, he said, "Bed hard." Another year passed and he came back to give a two-word summary to the monsignor. When asked the same question he said, "Food bad." The third year when he was asked what he had to say about the monastery he said, "I quit." To that response the monsignor said, "Well, I'm not surprised because all you've done is complain since you've been here."

Complaining, murmuring, and griping pretty well defined the construct of my life until I was thirty years old. Even though I may not have verbalized it, I still felt sorry for myself, and that was the movie playing in the background of my life. I was a victim rather than a victor in my mind's eye. Life was all about me and the victim I portrayed myself as.

I had no deep lasting joy in my life—because to have joy you have to get your priorities straight. The lineup for joy is nestled in the acronym JOY. Jesus, Others, Yourself is the order. All I had at this point was the fleshly trinity also known as me, me, and more of me. Narcissus was the controlling hero in my life at this moment in time.

Psychologists tell us there are two things necessary for human beings to be fulfilled and healthy in life. The first is significance and the second vital possession is security. *Significance* says, "I am somebody. I have value and worth." *Security* says, "I am safe and belong and fit in." That same old boa constrictor of bitterness, guilt, shame, and unforgiveness was choking every ounce of significance and security right out of me. In my heart I still felt responsible for my father's untimely death, and my heart ached that I wasn't speaking to him at the time of his unexpected exodus from this earth. Fear was still one of the paralyzing forces in my life. I had an epidemic of major fears. Fear of rejection, fear of failure, fear of punishment, and shame or hopelessness made a gradual crescendo in my life. I felt as if I were on a perpetual performance treadmill trying to measure up according to human standards to gain significance and security. I had not discovered at this point that *who you are* is much more important than *what you do* and that genuine significance and security come only by identifying with Jesus Christ as Lord.[6]

When you have bitterness, guilt, shame, unforgiveness, and rage roaring in your heart,

---

6   Many of the thoughts in this and the following two paragraphs are based on the following book and study we have taught for years: Robert McGee, *Search for Significance* (Nashville: Thomas Nelson, 2003).

it's difficult to focus on purpose and meaning. Perhaps that's why my heart had trouble adjusting to any one profession. By the time I was thirty years old, I had tried on so many professional hats that my head was sore and spinning. I had been a licensed schoolteacher, a realtor, an insurance agent, and a manager of a piano store before opening my own piano studio, where I would teach professionally for the next twenty-three years. During the same time frame, I sold real estate at my mama's real estate company.

I had served faithfully as church pianist in a Baptist church since before my conversion to Christ, but I felt the Lord calling me deeper and deeper into His service. I visited with a friend in another church one evening, and the Lord Jesus Christ, the Second Person of the Holy Trinity, graciously baptized me with His Holy Spirit, who is the Third Person of the Holy Trinity (Matthew 3:11; Mark 1:8; Luke 3:16; John 1:33). It was a fresh baptism of pure, unconditional love and acceptance.

The Third Person of the Holy Trinity, the Holy Spirit, had already baptized me into Jesus, the Second Person of the Trinity, at salvation when I was born again of the Holy Spirit (1 Corinthians 12:13).

Now with this new baptism the burning desire of my heart was to serve the Lord full time because empowerment for service is one of the main products of the baptism in or with the Holy Spirit. The first product of the baptism with the Holy Spirit was a passionate desire to obey the Lord and to live a life of holiness. Living proof of the resurrection of Jesus was the most outstanding evidence for me personally and a baptism of pure agape love.

Did I believe that was a one-time filling station never to be visited again? No indeed, because we are told to be constantly filled and refilled with the Third Person of the Holy Trinity. Did I believe in a second blessing? Absolutely. And a third, fourth, fifth blessing and infinitely more blessings for the asking. Our picture of God is too small. We need to expand our man-sized prayers and ask the Lord to give us God-sized prayers and accompany them with the faith to see our prayers accomplished.

At salvation I had been baptized into Jesus, but now Jesus had baptized me with the Holy Spirit and empowered me for service in His kingdom. This was a monumental launching pad for many excursions into the deep as I joined Jesus in the work He was doing.

The Lord really has a great sense of humor. I can remember times in college when I would accompany on the piano an opera singer and dear friend who later performed with the San Francisco Opera. I used to travel with her as her accompanist. Her father was a Pentecostal preacher, and occasionally I would accompany her for fun to this little Pentecostal church just to play the piano for her. Mostly I would go to laugh at the people in the church who spoke in tongues and danced in the Holy Spirit. I thought they were hilarious to watch. Well, looking back on my foolish laughter, it appears the Lord got the last laugh. My perspective now has changed dramatically as I reflect back, thinking what a precious little Holy-Ghost-filled congregation that was and how blessed I was to be allowed to experience the sweet flow of the Lord.

No more laughing at the things of God or the people of God for me. I may not have agreed one hundred percent with the theology, but I surely did agree with the move of the Holy Spirit and the respectful sincerity of worship there. I believe many things are only fluff or don't really matter enough to argue about theologically (issues that never affect your salvation and only cause schisms in the body of Christ). I discovered early on that the major concern is to seek the Giver and not the gifts of the Holy Spirit. I consider the Giver of the Holy Spirit to be the most magnificent Gift.

In 1978 I was accepted into graduate school at the Church of God Seminary in Cleveland, Tennessee, where I pursued a master's degree. I was the only woman in my classes and absolutely the only Baptist. My colleagues all enjoyed kidding me about my eternal security. I just ignored the loving harassment and focused on my studies, knowing in my heart that God my Father held my salvation tightly in His big strong hands and that no one could ever pluck me out of His hands. How does one get unborn after being born into a family? How does one get disinherited after being chosen, adopted, and called? How does the glue of your salvation come unsealed after the Holy Spirit seals you?

If I hold my own salvation in my finite hands, then I am more than limited and in big trouble. But I had placed my full faith and confidence in

Jesus Christ as the Highest Lord and in the work He did on the cross—not in my own feeble labors. This is not cheap grace being discussed, where you accept Jesus and then keep on living like hell. No, to be truly born again of the Holy Spirit, baptized into Jesus, and baptized by Jesus into the Holy Spirit and filled to overflowing means I am not saved by my works but by grace through faith. I still commit all my works to the Lord under His supervision and anointing. I am not saved by my works but saved to do good works because of the undying love I have for the Lord Jesus, my Heavenly Father, and the Holy Spirit.

My seminary brothers who challenged me were a blessing because being the brunt of their jokes made me search deeper for the truths in God's Word. I have some allergies to perfume and cologne, and the suffering I encountered didn't come from being ragged about my doctrine. The suffering came for me as I had to sit with these guys ten hours a day in closed-up classrooms. I mean, these seminary guys smelled like a French brothel because they obviously baptized themselves in deadly cologne every morning. One whiff of their aroma was anathema—abhorrent and odious to my allergic nostrils and immune system. It seems one of their favorite colognes was called "Eternity." One whiff of that stuff and boy howdy—it made me feel like I was on my way to eternity instantly. I felt so sorry for their wives and prayed they all had oxygen masks at home to keep them from being asphyxiated from the lethal aromas.

Throughout my tenure in seminary I was able to ignore all the pomp and circumstance, pontification, and ecclesiastical politics that echoed from my brothers in three-piece suits. I just continued to drive my baby-blue Jeep Wrangler convertible with denim top and wore my very casual, simple, light-blue-and-white seersucker dresses with no earrings because earrings were taboo in 1978 in this denomination. Even though I didn't wear those earrings physically, you can bet your bottom dollar I was wearing those earrings every day in my heart. I never felt it was wrong to wear earrings, but I did feel it was wrong to offend my brothers in Christ.

One thing I had decided was my calling from the Lord was more important than some manmade title. I set my heart like flint to choose *calling* over *title* every time. Why? Because titles breed entitlement and callings produce humility and servanthood. Titles are manmade, and callings are God-ordained. If Jesus Christ, the Creator and Sustainer of everything, could make Himself of no reputation and take up His cross, so could I. I decided early on that I would be Jesus' secret service minister with the goal of glorifying the Father rather than trying to please all men. I don't need to read *reverend* before my name as long as I know I am revered by the Lord of Glory. Like many manmade ministers, I do not have spiritual amnesia because I very clearly remember it was Mary whom Jesus called first to proclaim news of His resurrection. I just cannot understand why so many cannot figure out that the devil early on attempted to cut God's workforce in half by eliminating women as sounding boards for the Good News. Please do not think I am an advocate for women's lib because I am not, but I *am* a Jesus Lib Advocate.

My first semester in seminary I made a 4.0 grade-point average, even though I had no undergraduate degree in biblical studies. If this sounds like bragging, it is. I am bragging on the Lord Jesus Christ, who does amazing work. Anything good accomplished in my life was all

Jesus. Anything bad in my life was orchestrated and carried out by me apart from Jesus. I was so excited about the Lord Jesus and His Word I couldn't get enough of either. I was currently teaching sixty piano students a week and selling real estate, as well as attending seminary from nine a.m. until nine p.m. two days a week and often studying all night.

One of my favorite classes in seminary was "Preaching and Teaching with Purpose." I loved Professor May and his very dry but hysterical sense of humor. One day he entered our classroom laughing uncontrollably. We were wondering about his sanity until he shared with us that he had just listened to a mountain preacher on his car radio delivering a sermon on the subject of Phillip and the Ethiopian "UNCH." Of course, the preacher had a little problem pronouncing *eunuch*. Our class of all males, except for yours truly, joined our professor in roaring out of control with laughter.

It was during this class that my initial speaking engagement was assigned: Silverdale Women's Prison. The Lord has such a sense of humor because I hate germs and avoid them like the plague. I struggled in deciding on my sermon topic, but one thing was for sure: I knew I wasn't going to speak on the subject of Phillip and the Ethiopian "UNCH." The night I was scheduled to speak at the prison one of the inmates had stolen a potato peeler out of the kitchen, and it was never recovered. My prayer was "Lord, please don't let me become Miss Potato Head tonight." Another inmate, who had more body piercings and tattoos than seemed humanly possible, appeared to be demon possessed and pretended to speak in tongues and interrupted the entire time I spoke.

At least this first speaking engagement was not boring. And no, I didn't close my eyes during the prayers. My entire sermon lasted only about eight minutes, which is the dream of most nominal church goers. It was short and to the point, and miraculously several women gave their hearts to Christ that night, so it was worth the stress and strain. To God be all the glory!

Chapter 6

JEHOVAH-JIREH, MY PROVIDER

And Abraham called the name of the place, The-Lord-Will-Provide; as it is said to this day, "In the mount of the Lord it shall be provided."

— GENESIS 22:14

My next ministry assignment was as a volunteer chaplain at Memorial Hospital in Chattanooga. You guessed it—there were many more germs to contend with. At the same time, I completed a chaplaincy course at Erlanger Hospital and was assigned to minister at Children's Hospital, the official germ factory of the world. I was the only chaplain whose Bible was washed after rounds.

It was during this tenure I realized I needed a partner to spend my life with, and I began to pray for a husband. Five long years I prayed fervently asking the Lord to provide me with the mate of His choosing.

Every morning I met with God for a quiet time to receive the instructions He had for me that day. I developed this model from the Lord Jesus Christ because He also met with His Father every morning—in fact, the Heavenly Father woke him for that meeting.

> *"The Lord God has given Me the tongue of the learned, That I should know how to speak A word in season to him who is weary. He awakens Me morning by morning, He awakens My ear to hear as the learned."*
>
> — ISAIAH 50:4

One morning in my quiet time the Lord gave me a rhema word from Genesis 22:14 assuring me that He was Jehovah-Jireh, the Lord My Provider. This very same day when I arrived at Memorial Hospital to do my chaplain rounds, I met the man God had provided for me and had reserved for me from eternity past. Fewer than four hours after receiving that rhema word, I encountered the most gorgeous hunk of a man one could ever imagine.

It was this prayer for a husband that formally introduced me to Jehovah-Jireh, the Lord my Provider. Go with me, please, to Memorial Hospital to the second floor, known as One North, and turn right down the hallway, and let's knock on the door of the room midway down the hall. Ready? Here we go inside.

His masculine, silver-gray, crew cut hair, impeccably smooth olive complexion, and gorgeous brown eyes arrested my gaze as I entered his hospital room to offer a prayer and word of encouragement. It was most unusual to find such a genteel man with a six-foot six frame resembling that of an all-American football star yet reflecting the sweetness and humility of a gentle servant.

As a thirty-two-year-old hospital chaplain and senior seminary student, I knew any patient on One North at Memorial Hospital was critically, if not terminally, ill. How could any man who looked so handsome be so ill? I soon discovered as Sister Rose, the visiting nun, introduced me to him that he was a forty-two-year-old bachelor suffering from complications of surgery. He had massive blood clots in both lungs and was a living, breathing miracle to still be alive.

I offered a prayer for his healing and then immediately ran downstairs to my office to call a friend on the phone to ask for a prayer of agreement that this hunk of a man would invite me out on a date. After hanging up the phone, I did something I had never done before—I went back to his room. When I walked in, he had a piece of hard candy stuck to the roof of his mouth and was unable to speak. I quickly sputtered out the words, "Well, I came back to tell you I'm leaving now." Before I could finish my sentence, he freed himself from the candy and asked if I would like to go fishing with him sometime. I loved to fish, but I loved to look at this fisherman most of all, so I told him I'd love to go fishing with him. I found out later that when his father heard of this meeting, he commented, "Looks like she's caught a big one this time."

I was frantic because he was being dismissed from the hospital early the next morning, and I was afraid he would forget to call me. I decided to send him a get-well card. Actually, I bought seven cards, each one with an apple on it. You know the old saying "An apple a day keeps the doctor away." I wanted only to keep the other women away because I soon discovered there was an available nurse on One North who also thought Mr. Sanders was an impressive catch. I sent seven apples and seven days of scriptures to Mr. Jimmy D. Sanders in Jasper, Tennessee. I planted an engraved pocket-sized New Testament in the seventh apple card just in case he forgot what I did at the hospital. His mother later told me that after the first card arrived, every day about the time the mailman would pass, Mr. Jimmy D. Sanders would walk to the mailbox in his pajamas like a child waiting for the ice-cream wagon just to wait for the next apple-a-day card.

My plan must have worked because, sure enough, about a week after the last apple card arrived, I received a phone call from him inviting me out on a date. This old maid and that old bachelor went out every Friday, Saturday, and Sunday evening. On our very first date we attended a barbershop quartet concert at the Tivoli Theatre. One of my dear friends, Betty McKeehan, had invited us because her husband, Bill, sang tenor in a quartet. Mrs. Betty had been my junior-high-school typing teacher and was someone I cherished and adored. She had loved, accepted, and mentored me at a crucial time in my life when I didn't know where to turn. Even though she was extremely busy with her job, family, and church, she slowed down and bent down to help me find my way up in life. Mrs. Betty was an impeccable role model of what a Christian mother should look like. We enjoyed thirty-five years of a precious God-ordained friendship.

After the concert Jimmy and I returned to my home, where we talked until the wee hours of the morning about Jimmy's service in Vietnam. Uncle Sam drafted him when he was twenty-five years old. It seems he had never ventilated to anyone the traumatic yet silent emotional and mental wounds he had received in the war. He said when he returned home from the service he could not sleep so he would just get in his car and drive all night. He went back to work and held a regular job but the painful scars on his mind tormented him with night terrors, survivor's guilt, deep sadness, and horrible flashbacks just like those my daddy had suffered from World War II. One very different yet tragic symptom of the Vietnam War was the shame he endured because of an ungrateful nation. He just could not grasp the fact that he had gone to Southeast Asia and slept on rice paddies with snakes crawling over him at night and Vietnamese shooting at him as he fought for the United States of America and then returned home to a nation that blamed the innocent soldiers for what they declared as a useless war. The physical traumas he suffered included high blood pressure, gastric upset that did not dissipate, and hundreds of skin cancers from being sprayed with Agent Orange. The great news of this story is that Jimmy never saw himself as a victim but always as a victor. He had fought a good fight for his country even if the country did not return the favor. The amazing thing was he passionately loved his country and held no animosity toward the ignorant, indignant population who protested the war and blamed the innocent war heroes.

The commonality of Jimmy's war record and my nocturnal family battles with a war veteran of World War II was one of many wonderful constructs upon which we built an enduring relationship. Certainly, the most prominent foundation was our relationship to Jesus Christ as our Commander in Chief. We dated for several years and enjoyed many fishing, hiking, and deer hunting outings. One of our favorite dates was ministering to the homeless population in Miller Park.

Three years and three engagement rings later, we were married by the same minister who had led me to Christ when I tracked him down at Sambo's Restaurant. Our wedding congregation looked like a flock of penguins had settled over that small Baptist church on Hickory Valley Road in East Brainerd. I mean every nun at Memorial Hospital was there—prim, proper, and proud as punch—claiming credit for the introduction. It was a very sweet gathering with the Lord Jesus Christ postured right in the center of all the festivities.

Since my Daddy Jim had already graduated to the balcony and was unavailable to walk me down the aisle, the Lord Jesus had arranged for me to meet a wonderful family several years earlier who owned a Bible bookstore. The Gaithers were special friends. Waymon Gaither, the father, walked me down the aisle and gave me away. I was lovingly titled from that day on as his "giveaway girl." As a prelude to the service, Waymon sang "The Lord's Prayer" and his wife, Sue, played the organ for the service. Our processional was the hymn "Great Is Thy Faithfulness." Little did we know this relationship would blossom into a treasured lifetime friendship with the Gaithers.

Chapter 7

HEALING OF SPIRIT, SOUL, AND BODY

Let all bitterness, wrath, anger, clamor, and evil speaking be put away from you, with all malice. And be kind to one another, tenderhearted, forgiving one another, even as God in Christ forgave you.

— EPHESIANS 4:31–32

Immediately following our ten o'clock morning wedding service and reception we were stressed to the max. We went home to our two-bedroom apartment on Concord Road in East Brainerd and went to bed and slept for six hours.

Before we collapsed into bed that day, I was literally in shock when my new husband came out of the bathroom in his red plaid pajamas and smiled at me. Who was this man? Jimmy forgot to tell me he had an upper partial dental plate right in front where he smiled so boldly. He was missing his three upper front teeth. Glory to God, at that moment all I could think of was the song "All I Want for Christmas Is My Two Front Teeth." I am not sure that's what the scripture in Psalm 81:10 meant when God said, "Open your mouth wide, and I will fill it."

We decided in advance that we would delay our honeymoon four months and go trout fishing in the fall on the Tellico River in Tellico Plains and then head up to Gatlinburg, Tennessee, and catch all the fish we could there. The first workday after our wedding I expected my new husband to show up late in the middle of the night after work just as my daddy had always done. Jimmy got off work at three-thirty in the afternoon. I almost passed out cold when he arrived home at ten minutes after four in the afternoon. He continued this posture of faithfulness his entire working career. The Lord God Almighty knew I needed stability, constancy, and a husband of impeccable integrity to help with the daily healing process in my life.

I would love to pretend right here and say that we lived happily ever after, but in all honesty we did drive off into a few Grand Canyons along our married journey. When we arrived back in Chattanooga after our honeymoon of trout fishing, the honeymoon seemed to be over. I was totally spoiled, and Jimmy was totally a bachelor at heart, so I got up one morning and decided to file for divorce. I told him that if he didn't quit slurping his coffee and continued to refuse to eat the broccoli I cooked, I was going to divorce him. He simply replied, "I'm not giving you a divorce because I made a commitment to God Almighty."

One other thing really made me angry with him: he told me he quit chewing tobacco, but I discovered a huge bag of Red Man in his pocket. When he arrived home that afternoon, I had nailed that bag of Red Man to the bedroom wall right smack dab over our bed. We would go to church on Sunday and I would sit on one side of the church and he would sit on the opposite side.

I actually did get brave and hired an attorney and filed for divorce one morning. And yes, I spent Jimmy's three hundred dollars for the legal fees. Late that afternoon after I had divorce papers served on him at his job, the Lord spoke to me. I felt that He said, "If you go through with this divorce, your ministry is over."

I believed the Lord and so I went home that night and begged Jimmy to forgive me. Of course, he did—instantly. Two very godly married couples counseled Jimmy and me and prayed with us until we were stable enough to continue on in this journey called marriage. However, some twenty years later one of the ladies we ministered to in our small group at church who was a private investigator came into our Sunday morning congregation and announced she had seen on the courthouse records that I had filed for a divorce. It was a little uncomfortable, but I did confess my mistake.

It was a common practice for my new husband to hold me in his arms and pray many prayers asking the Lord to heal the memories of my fractured childhood. Finally I recognized the stumbling block preventing healing all hinged around one word—*forgiveness*. I had unforgiveness against my earthly father and also my Heavenly Father, as well as myself. I knew the Bible says communicating with the dead is against God's laws, but the Holy Spirit revealed to me that I could talk to Jesus and Jesus could share my heart with my deceased father.

One afternoon in early spring my husband took me over to my father's grave, where he left me for an extended period of time so I could experience some healing. I spent my time talking to Jesus and sharing my anger, bitterness, grief, regrets, and charges against my father. I verbally listed every offense and every injury my father had inflicted upon me, and I made a quality decision to forgive my daddy of every offense and every injury because Jesus had forgiven me of all of my offenses and injuries. I truly wanted to obey Ephesians 4:31–32 that mandates this: "Let all bitterness, wrath, anger, clamor, and evil speaking be put away from you, with all malice. And be kind to one another, tenderhearted, forgiving one another, even as God in Christ forgave you."

The Word of God in Matthew 18:21–35 states that for genuine forgiveness to occur it must be given from the heart and not just from an exterior remote posture. My heart truly ached and longed to forgive my earthly daddy and my Heavenly Daddy from my heart. I simply asked Jesus to let my earthly father know I had forgiven him and was releasing him from all offenses. In that same meeting I also forgave Jesus and myself.

So many people who embrace unforgiveness refuse to do the three simple steps of the forgiveness process because it's easier to hold on to bitterness or to excuse away the offense or injury by saying it really wasn't that bad. These three steps are necessary for heartfelt forgiveness to take place: First, an offense takes place; second, an injury results from the offense; and third, after acknowledging the offense and injury, the choice is made to forgive the sinner and release them as Jesus has forgiven and released us.

Step one is so very significant because many people ignore offenses and deny and repress the truth of being offended. Why do they do this? It's much easier to ignore the truth and pretend it just never happened in order to avoid step two and the pain that occurs from the injury. If step one is denied, then there will never be an admission of step two and the injury that resulted from the offense. This is like putting a Band-Aid on a gunshot wound or doing nothing at all to the wound. Sooner or later an infection is going to set up and finally erupt and cause systemic trauma to the body. Spiritual and emotional healing can take place only when all three steps of the forgiveness process are practiced from the heart.

When I engaged in forgiving my father, my Lord, and myself, the heavy weight of sin just lifted from my grieving heart. Freedom was mine at last! I was convinced beyond a shadow of a doubt that forgiveness is a stepping-stone to promotion from the Lord.

That boa constrictor of hatred, bitterness, shame, condemnation, unforgiveness, and rage had finally been cut and removed from my soul by the sword of God's Word. Now my problem of yesterday had become my platform for ministry today and forever. I could now freely share the same comfort I had received from the Holy Spirit when I talked with others struggling in the same areas.

I sensed the influence of Narcissus finally fading into the background. As a matter of fact, I chose to kiss Narcissus good-bye and bury that haughty, prideful, selfish spirit right there in Greenwood Cemetery next to my Daddy Jim that day.

I made another monumental decision at that point. I decided I was no longer to appraise myself as a victim of my past and wallow in self-pity. Now my new identity in Christ was titled *victor*. The poem "Self-Pity" by D. H. Lawrence became very precious to me. Here's what it says: "I never saw a wild thing sorry for itself. A small bird will drop frozen dead from a bough without ever having felt sorry for itself."[7] There are three key words in this poem: *sorry for itself*. These words convey the simple message that self-pity is self-consuming and usually self-destructive. As I left the cemetery that day, I thanked the Lord for receiving my self-pity in His body on the cross in exchange for my new victorious posture that overcomes the world, the flesh, and the devil.

Thirteen months after we were married, I gave birth to a precious baby girl. We thought she was going to be a James, but we were pleasantly surprised with our new baby girl, Mary Anna, who weighed seven pounds, seven ounces. She was the most beautiful child I had ever seen. Holding Mary Anna for the first time was the

---

7   D. H. Lawrence, "Self-Pity," *The Complete Poems of D. H. Lawrence* (Ware, Hertfordshire, England: Wordsworth Editions Limited, 1994).

greatest miracle of life I had ever experienced. God had truly graced us with a treasure of all treasures.

Four months after Mary Anna was born, I became very ill with complications of the C-section. I suddenly began coughing up blood and was rushed to the hospital, where I was diagnosed with a pulmonary embolus. My doctor said it was a silent blood clot resulting from the C-section. This diagnosis was documented by a lung scan on Friday. Saturday afternoon I was visited by my dear friend Jo Ann, who had served as matron of honor in my wedding. She came with great faith and anointed me with oil as James 5:14–16 instructs. When she prayed, I sensed the power and presence of the Holy Spirit and believed in my heart that God had healed me. This belief was confirmed on Monday when another lung scan was done—and showed no sign of a blood clot.

Medical science struggles with miracles, so my lung specialist suggested that maybe the initial diagnosis had been wrong, but I knew who had touched me and healed me. He was the same God who had kept me safe as a child, provided a magnificent husband for me, given me a perfect, beautiful daughter, and placed a calling on my life that had given me purpose and meaning. Now at the age of thirty-six I had experienced what Isaiah 53:5 declares—that Jesus was indeed wounded for my transgressions, bruised for my iniquities, the chastisement for my peace was upon Jesus, and by His stripes I was healed.

Thank God I was healed spiritually, emotionally, mentally, and physically. The Greek word for *salvation* is *sozo*, which means "wholeness and well-being in every area of life." Now I knew what *sozo* meant experientially.

Chapter 8

LAUNCHING OUT
INTO THE DEEP

*"Launch out into the deep and let down
your nets for a catch."*

—LUKE 5:4

The next ten years my husband and I served as an elder team at City Church of Chattanooga. Our pastor, Dr. Mike Chapman, and his wife, Trudy, believed in the doctrine of the priesthood of believers and equipping the saints for the work of the ministry and then releasing them into the fields white for harvest.

We taught multiple Bible classes and I even taught some seminary courses during this tenure. We both sensed the Lord drawing us more deeply in the direction of ministry for our community. We had just completed facilitating a class by Henry Blackaby titled "Experiencing God."[8] The thrust of that course was we could experience God fully if we would join Him in the work He was doing rather than asking Him to join us in our feeble fleshly endeavors.

While fasting and praying about where to serve, I sensed the Holy Spirit instructing me to read the want ads in the newspaper. I argued with the Lord at first but then finally opened the Chattanooga newspaper and noticed a small ad for a volunteer pianist at a downtown men's inner-city homeless mission. I called the Maranatha Rescue Mission and agreed to play the piano for their evening services one night a week.

When preparing to go the first evening, I sensed the Lord urging me to take a sermon along. Again I argued with the Lord, saying a Baptist mission would never let a woman deliver a sermon. I finally agreed to take a sermon along with my music, and I also packed up my husband to accompany me.

---

8   Henry Blackaby and Claude King, *Experiencing God: Knowing and Doing the Will of God* (Nashville: Holman Publishers, 1990).

I always try to operate under the headship of my husband. That evening the preacher did not show up, so Jim and I delivered the sermon. The title of our message was "How to Be Satisfied," and the text was John 4 about the woman at the well. Nine men gave their hearts to Jesus that evening. I had trouble believing that so many wanted to accept Jesus, so I had them raise their right hand, then their left hand, then their right foot and left foot just to make sure. I guess we made them do the hokey pokey and turn themselves around just to prove their sincerity. To God be all the glory; great things He has done!

My husband and I ministered at that mission for the next two years: preaching, leading music, and learning about the homeless population. We realized from our experience there that Chattanooga did not have a Christ-centered homeless mission shelter for women and children. After a great deal of prayer, in October 1995 we joined the Lord in His work by forming a board of directors and founding the Shepherd's Arms Rescue Mission for homeless women with children. The founding scripture the Lord gave us was Proverbs 24:11—"Rescue those being led away to death; hold back those staggering toward slaughter" (NIV).

The Lord gave us a word that we were not to borrow money but to wait and allow Him to provide what was needed. We promised the Lord we would not borrow money but would wait on Him to supply our needs. We also knew we were never to accept any government funding because we did not wish to compromise the biblical posture of the ministry.

The ministry was launched with $1,000 from the small group we led at City Church of Chattanooga. We worked from our home office for the first two years with no salary the first eighteen months and very little salary the next two years. During the first two years we spoke in fifty churches casting the vision the Lord had given us. We also wrote twenty grant proposals trying to secure funding to purchase our first 5,900-square-foot church building in Alton Park.

After two years the Lord supplied $75,000 to purchase the building and provided another $30,000 to repair it. Almost every window in the chapel had been shot out by bullets. There was a lot of water standing in the building, and it took us a very long time to remove all the beer and whiskey bottles. We had initially told the Lord we would go anywhere He wanted except we did not want to go to Alton Park. It's amazing how the Lord knows exactly what is best. The church building we purchased in Alton Park proved to be the best location we could have imagined.

We didn't just storm right into the neighborhood and set up a ministry. First, we visited every home in a two-mile radius asking if the neighbors wanted us in their community. We were given the blessings of the neighborhood except for one elderly lady who followed us to city hall to protest our rezoning. This lady lived directly in front of the mission. She blasted us for thirty minutes before the city commission. Following her irate protest my husband spoke only five minutes and we were approved unanimously. Little did we know this same lady would learn to love us and even ask us to help her take care of her property when she was out of town. After her death we purchased her home and joyfully restored it like new, and it now serves as a ministry residence.

At the age of forty-seven I had given up my professional piano studio and real estate business to become a full-time home missionary in Alton Park. Jim was fifty-seven years old at the time and worked five more years at Combustion Engineering before joining me in the work full-time at Shepherd's Arms. We were both so excited about joining the Lord full-time in the work He was doing among homeless women and children, widows, and at-risk inner-city youth.

The first convert to Christ at Shepherd's Arms was a man delivering lumber for repairs of the building. The lavish provision the Lord showered upon us was so inspiring to our faith. One Saturday we were painting the chapel and a retired professor from Missouri University came in saying he wanted to make a donation. We thought it might be some clothes or furniture. To our great surprise he gave us a house and two lots adjoining the mission property. That property housed our clothes ministry for several years. Then ten years later we demolished the house and made a sweet peaceful park where our ladies and children could sit outside and enjoy nature.

At the end of the first fiscal year we were $10,000 in the red on our annual budget. Anxiety began to well up inside us until the Holy Spirit brought a marvelous scripture to our minds. This powerful word says, "Be anxious for nothing, but in everything by prayer and supplication with thanksgiving, let your requests be made known to God" (Philippians 4:6). That's just exactly what we did. We told no one about the need but went into the chapel and got on our faces before the Lord, thanking Him for being our Father and asking for $10,000. At the same time a doctor on Lookout Mountain was praying and the Lord led him to send us $10,000, which we received in the mail the very next day. The exact same thing happened the following year when we were $10,000 short again and the Lord had someone send us exactly $10,000 the next day.

The Lord has never been late to supply every need for us personally and for His mission at Shepherd's Arms.

Chapter 9

FLYING THE FLAG OF ACCEPTANCE

And let us consider how we may spur one another on toward love and good deeds.
— HEBREWS 10:24 NIV

We had just moved into the building in Alton Park where the new mission was being established when I caught a glimpse of her tall, strong, African-American frame walking up the steep hill to our parking lot. I kept straining to see what she was carrying in her arms, but she was too far away. The closer she came, the predominant colors of red, white, and blue began to shine more brightly.

I had never seen this woman before, but she had

come out of a house near the mission. As she entered our parking lot she said, "I just wanted to welcome you to the neighborhood. I am your neighbor." Then she handed my husband a very large, bold American flag and said, "I noticed you just put up a flagpole and I wanted to give you this flag if you will have it."

As we continued to talk, we discovered this flag was the one that had been placed upon her veteran husband's coffin. She had saved it for many years for just this moment. That flag was very precious to her heart but now even more so to ours. This was the best possible welcoming gesture of love and acceptance we could ever think of receiving.

We discovered her name was Mrs. Smith and she was almost seventy years old. She had lived a very challenging life. One of her daughters had been tragically killed simultaneously with her grandchild. Another daughter was mentally ill and had to be monitored day and night. She had one son on death row and another son in prison for lesser charges.

Mrs. Smith began to attend our chapel services and in just a few weeks she accepted Jesus as her Lord. My husband baptized Mrs. Smith and her daughter during the first baptismal service we held. It was Jim's first experience baptizing so I cringed when he held the first candidate under water too long—unintentionally, of course. She came up kicking! If she hadn't been a true believer when she went under the water, she for certain was when she surfaced. He did a much better job with the second candidate.

The mission had just started a program to help clients get their GEDs (general equivalency diplomas). Mrs. Smith signed up as our first student. She was seventy years old when she completed her GED program and received her diploma. A picture of her in her handsome cap and gown still plays as a treasured memory in my mind.

It wasn't very long until Mrs. Smith began to cook for the mission. She was a skilled cook, and our residents enjoyed the blessings of her labors. Chicken and dumplings and pancakes were her specialties. She cooked for the ministry for many years and also served as a supply housemother. Her role model of acceptance, love, and generosity encouraged all the staff, volunteers, and residents at Shepherd's Arms. Her husband's flag was proudly flown over this mission until it became tattered and torn, but her kindness, compassion, and acceptance are still flown over this mission every day.

Chapter 10

EGREGIOUSLY SURPRISING POPULATION

And the Lord God said, "Behold, the man is become as one of Us, to know good and evil.

— GENESIS 3:22

We were thrilled to be nestled in between two famous Civil War battlefields. Shepherd's Arms was in the valley between Lookout Mountain and Missionary Ridge. Even though the Civil War ended April 9, 1865, in the valley where we were located, there was another battle raging spiritually between good and evil. John Milton, author of *Paradise Lost*,[9] might have been shocked and surprised by the depth of spiritual depravity raging in this valley. Adam and

Eve blew it big time in the Garden of Eden and lost their home in paradise after disobeying God and buying into Satan's lies, but thank God, Jesus Christ purchased paradise back with His own blood on Calvary's cross.

The stats on crime and poverty in the Alton Park Area in 1997 were the highest in the city of Chattanooga. Drug addicts, dealers, and prostitutes lined the sidewalks just one block from the newly established mission. Every Sunday our chapel services were filled with a wide variety of professional lifetime criminals. Almost every congregant had a newly posted mug shot on file at City Hall. The Lord was actively bringing them in and saving their souls.

The very first year over two hundred individuals made decisions at Shepherd's Arms Rescue Mission to follow Jesus Christ as Lord. We were thrilled we had joined Jesus in His exciting work of transformation. Now we were understanding what Henry Blackaby had taught us in his "Experiencing God" course. The Lord was all over this mission doing His marvelous works and we were just enjoying His presence as we watched Him at work.

My cousin Caroline graced us with the greatest compliment and word of encouragement as she just blurted out that when she and her family drove through Alton Park, they quickly locked all their car doors and accelerated their car because of fear . . . but the Sanders family drove into the middle of Alton Park, opened all their doors, and invited everyone to come in.

As you well know, life doesn't always circulate around the ceiling. During our tenure in Alton Park we experienced two extremely unconventional encounters with women of ill repute. The first of these encounters happened when a neighborhood woman rang the mission doorbell asking for a plate of food. We prepared a delicious food plate and gave it to her at the door. As she received the plate of food, she immediately demanded that we give her a second plate. We responded, "You haven't eaten this food yet. Just come back tomorrow and we will give you another plate." Our words must have set off the demonic alarm clock because she started cursing us as she walked down the steps, telling us to kiss her gluteus maximus. Well, actually she didn't say "gluteus maximus" but substituted the inner-city synonym for that body part that is often used to describe a donkey.

My husband and I were standing there with two African-American gentlemen when this woman surprised us by yelling, "Well, I can do one better" as she dropped her pants and mooned us right there on our parking lot. Good grief—I don't remember receiving any instruction in seminary about handling this kind of demonstration. My response was "Please just give the plate of food back." To that she quickly pulled up her pants and ran quickly away with her plate of food. After her roadrunner departure, we were speechless. This experience left us with a new appreciation for the statement "Silence is golden." We just looked at each other and smiled, pretending to hear no evil, see no evil, speak no evil.

These stories were egregiously surprising to us. The second encounter happened as my husband and I were teaching a new biblical series from the book of Proverbs. The topic this particular Sunday was "The Wise Woman in Contrast to the Boisterous Woman." After we read the scripture describing the loud, boisterous woman, one of our neighborhood prostitutes stood up and started to curse us, taking the Lord's name in vain, saying, "You G.D. preachers—you can't talk to me like that."

Wow! Once again I racked my brain to try to remember in my Church of God seminary classes if they ever instructed us in how to handle such a situation. The Word of God had obviously hit the bull's-eye as we spoke and accidentally poked the sleeping bear that immediately rose up to curse us. My "Preaching and Teaching with a Purpose" class never meant for this kind of literal application to erupt.

We tried to ignore it the first time it happened, but as we continued our message, she stood again and repeated the same words. It became necessary for us to escort her outside the building and ban her from attending chapel for the next three months. After three months she returned to service and once again stood up and interrupted the message, cursing us. This time we banned her for another three months, promising to ban her indefinitely if that ever happened again.

Our plan of action was to faithfully pray for this woman. We did so for the next fifteen years as she sporadically attended chapel services. One day we received news that she had experienced a series of serious health issues and was hospitalized after having five strokes. During her illness we visited her, prayed with her, and provided food and medications to help her. When she was physically able to attend chapel service again, she gave her heart to the Lord Jesus Christ. Now rather than cursing us and taking the name of the Lord in vain, she uses her voice to praise the name of the Lord, giving Him the honor and glory that is due Him. This precious lady has been faithful to serve the Lord now for many years and often shares her testimony with others.

Chapter 11

POPCORN, ANYONE?

"He who believes . . . will lay hands on the sick, and they will recover."

— MARK 16:16, 18

One bright, sunny afternoon we noticed a jet-black, very thin cocker spaniel hanging around the chapel doors. This poor dog was battered and bleeding and appeared to be half dead. My secretary immediately ran into the office and called the humane society to have the dog removed, but it was already too late because I had instantly fallen in love with this little fellow. Before the dogcatcher arrived, I hid the pooch inside my office. I just sensed the Lord had sent this disguised blessing to us and I couldn't ship him off to the dog pound.

We named this jet-black canine "Popcorn." After taking Popcorn to the veterinarian, we were told he had an incurable case of distemper and a nasty case of the mange. The vet doctored Popcorn for the mange but told us he would probably die very soon from the distemper.

Our mission children as well as our staff had also fallen head over heels in love with Popcorn. These homeless children had never had a father consistently present in their lives, much less a real pet. You know, the old saying that a dog is man's best friend is very true . . . and how true that statement became to our mission children.

Jesus says in Mark 16:18 that believers in Christ can lay hands on the sick and they will recover. We really never considered that this particular scripture just might apply to our four-legged friends, so we decided to try that practice with Popcorn. I mean, what could it hurt at this point to touch a dog and pray for him?

We gathered all the mission children around and read that scripture. Then we laid believing hands on Popcorn, praying and asking the Lord to please heal him. Let me say right here and now—children really and truly have faith to believe God and His Word because they haven't been around long enough to be taught unbelief. Sure enough, after that powerful, harmonious prayer, Popcorn started to feel much stronger. Every day our pup got stronger and stronger until he was one hundred percent new.

I had always believed the Lord heals every single time in one of three ways. He heals gradually as he did with Popcorn, He heals instantly as we prefer, or He heals ultimately as He invites us into His Father's house in heaven. The Lord answered our prayer and Popcorn lived another ten years and served faithfully as our mission mascot. The joy Popcorn brought to everyone at the mission was immeasurable. Doggone it, who would have ever believed Popcorn could bring such delight?

Chapter 12

MR. BEAR

Be diligent to present yourself approved to God, a worker who does not need to be ashamed, rightly dividing the word of truth.

— 2 TIMOTHY 2:15

Day after day our dogs—Popcorn, Noah, and Moses—would bark and jump up on the fence, informing us that he was slowly but surely inching up the steep hill by the mission. In my mind's eye I can still see his elderly, lanky, six-foot five-inch frame limping with a cane, trying to navigate the challenge before him. He always had on a pair of worn-out boots, faded overalls, an old-man flannel ball cap with flaps over the ears, and a well-worn plaid flannel shirt—no matter what the weather was outside. I finally mustered up enough courage to engage in a conversation with him while he was resting on his cane taking a breathing break. My first inquiry was to find out if he lived near the mission. He surely did, about one mile away in a two-story rental house. As our conversation progressed, I asked him if he would like to attend our Sunday afternoon chapel service at four o'clock. He very quickly and abruptly said no thanks. He said he wasn't a Christian and had no interest in becoming one.

Our conversation that day was the first of many because every time I heard the dogs bark, I would check to see if Mr. Bear was walking up the hill. His name was Billy, but his nickname was "Mr. Bear." I started greeting Mr. Bear with sweetcakes that he and Mrs. Bear could enjoy when he arrived home. Mr. Bear loved blueberry muffins and was totally crazy about banana-nut bread, so we were locked at the hip now by our sweetcakes. We finally started going to Mr. Bear's home and delivering sweet cakes every time we got a new supply. Every opportune moment we would lace all those sweet cakes with talk about the goodness of Jesus. Our conversations slowly but surely were transformed from idle superficial words to deeper spiritual issues.

One Sunday afternoon in our chapel service I was totally surprised to see Mr. Bear walking into the service in his faded overalls, ball cap, and well-worn plaid flannel shirt. He was eighty years old at that time and couldn't read or write, but he had a strong desire to learn. On the first Sunday of his attendance when the invitation to accept Jesus as Lord was given, Mr. Bear was the first one to raise his hand. He had already made up his mind before he arrived that day that Jesus was going to be his Lord and Savior. He wanted to become a Christian even though he couldn't read the Bible. His wife had been reading the Bible to Mr. Bear at home at night and it had paid off.

The next request of Mr. Bear was to ask us if we could teach him to read and write. We had a retired schoolteacher volunteering at the time, and she taught Mr. Bear how to write his name. I will never forget how excited Mr. Bear was the day he wrote his name for the very first time. I still have that cherished piece of paper with *Billy* written on it.

After Mr. Bear decided to follow Jesus, he never

missed a chapel service until his death. He was such a sweet inspiration to our congregation as he would always sing his prayers in a deep baritone voice. He would begin with a low humming and then begin to sing his inner-city blues version of "The Lawd's Prayer."

In his younger years he sang and played the guitar in a blues group, but he had stopped singing when one of his best friends in the group was shot and killed. He said he just lost his song and hadn't recovered it until he found Jesus.

When Mr. Bear graduated to the balcony, the family asked my husband to conduct his funeral, and, of course, he did. Mr. Bear taught us a marvelous lesson about never giving up on people because of their age or education.

Once again, we had experienced God in the remarkable life of Mr. Bear as we joined the Lord in the work He was doing.

Chapter 13

AN ANGEL UNAWARE?

Every good gift and every perfect gift is from above, and comes down from the Father of lights, with whom there is no variation or shadow of turning.

— JAMES 1:17

D o you believe in angels? I'm not talking about the ordinary spiritual brand of angels right now but the human kind that just simply show up unexpectedly and grace your life with blessings too numerous to count. I certainly believe in angels—both the spiritual kind and the earthly ones.

Oddly enough, these earthly angels sometimes

are so fragile and angelic in nature that they inadvertently get wounded, trampled underfoot, and almost destroyed by strong, insensitive task-oriented people. These sweet, kind, gentle angels of the human breed are masters at teaching the task performers of this world how important it is to be people oriented. The Lord enrolled me in one of these humility-building classes taught by a human angel, and I studied under her tutelage for thirteen years. Let me tell you about this non-elective school.

We had searched high and low for a new housemother at Shepherd's Arms Rescue Mission and had almost given up hope of filling the position when we received a call from Chicago from a lady who spoke very directly and with a more-than-Northern accent. This lady told us she was very much interested in the position and would like to relocate in the South because her brother lived in this area. She said her name was Katie and that she loved the Lord Jesus Christ with all her heart.

When Katie arrived in Chattanooga for her interview, the presence of God Almighty showed up ahead of her, announcing her arrival. When she walked into this mission, her countenance and personal appearance shouted MISSIONARY in all caps. If a neon sign had been flashing *Katie* on the screen, it could not have been any clearer that God had chosen and called this person to join Him in the work He was doing among homeless women and children at Shepherd's Arms. Katie may have been five feet tall on a wide stretch. She had jet black hair, and when she walked in with her charming red bucket rain hat and matching red plaid raincoat, sporting a tiny pair of Mary Jane shoes, she was a precious sight to behold. When she walked she had a slight limp because when she was born she had no hip sockets, but the Lord had healed her and now she was able to walk just fine.

Our staff fell instantly in love with Miss Katie. One look at Katie and you would never think anything but wall-to-wall joy and happiness were gifted to her because she was filled to overflowing with the love of Jesus. She gave two hundred percent to every project she tackled. What she did was not perfect in the eyes of staunch task-oriented people, but you could be sure it was more than perfect in the eyes of a compassionate, loving God who is people oriented and balanced in every way.

Talk about a prayer warrior—this tiny little lady, so small in stature, could soar with spiritual giants of any magnitude. When Katie opened her mouth and heart to pray, she literally stormed the gates of heaven. She unconditionally loved every homeless mother and child the Lord Jesus brought to Shepherd's Arms to reside. Katie taught every mother and child the words of Jeremiah 29:11. If you ask one of those residents twenty years later what Jeremiah 29:11 said, they would quote it and quickly tell you that Miss Katie had taught them that verse. Miss Katie literally believed what the Lord said in Jeremiah 29:11: "I know the thoughts that I think toward you, says the Lord, thoughts of peace and not of evil, to give you a future and a hope."

The children at the mission adored Miss Katie. In fact, no child ever wanted to leave the shelter after meeting her. Each child cherished her warm embrace and couldn't get enough of her totally corny but extremely cute jokes. The sweet thing about Katie's jokes was the belly laugh she attached to every one she shared.

Let me tell you now that Katie was a very literal woman. I remember coming into the dormitory area when the children were too loud and out of control and looking at Katie and jokingly telling her to run call the police and have these wild children arrested. The moment I mentioned the police, the children instantly became silent and well behaved. I turned around to tell Miss Katie that the children were behaving now and noticed she was nowhere to be found. About three minutes later she came back into the dorm area out of breath. When I inquired where she had been, I was told she had hurriedly called the police. Thankfully we were able to cancel the call before the police arrived and arrested me and Katie.

During the thirteen years of her tenure we experienced dozens of her literal obedience reactions. Unfortunately, I did not always see the humor in them. Because of my stubborn hardheadedness Katie and I tangled like sisters more often than we should. My task-oriented posture often trampled underfoot her people-oriented love, kindness, and faithfulness. It's so sad that in life we are such slow learners of the most important things and miss the blessings of the moment.

Sadly, Katie was gone by the time I fully learned what she was teaching me about God's priorities and spiritual maturity. One Friday afternoon I received a phone call from one of our board members saying Katie had been involved in a horrible car accident on the interstate highway and had been declared brain dead by the doctors. My husband and daughter rushed to the hospital ICU and held her tiny hand and prayed with her. Even though I had been a hospital chaplain at three different hospitals, I could not make my traumatized body go to see her. After her adopted son arrived in town from Chicago, Miss Katie was taken off life support and made her abundant entrance into heaven.

I believe Katie taught me as much as anyone could about what's really important in life. After she was translated into heaven, I realized the depth of love I felt for her and the deep sense of respect I had for her even though I rarely expressed either of those things to her fully while she was alive because I was too busy trying to get all the tasks completed perfectly. It's not as important to have perfect work projects as it is to treat people with kindness, respect, and love while giving each person space to grow into the image of Jesus Christ more perfectly.

Katie tried to teach me how not to wound the precious little mockingbirds around me. She was a great teacher on how I should practice and learn how to perfectly kiss Narcissus good-bye. I wish everyone could have the joy of going to a humility school taught by an earthly angel like Katie.

Sometimes the most valuable and gigantic heavenly blessings are dressed in red bucket rain hats, sporting red plaid raincoats, and wearing Mary Jane slippers. Be sure to keep your eye out for them—because sometimes you just might be entertaining an earthly angel unaware.

Chapter 14

A FATHERLY EMBRACE

"If you then, being evil, know how to give good gifts to your children, how much more will your Father who is in heaven give good things to those who ask Him!"

— MATTHEW 7:11

Every day we learned to trust Jesus more as our provider. We had studied the ministry of George Mueller and his wife, who founded the Ashley Down Orphanage in Bristol, England, where more than ten thousand orphans were cared for. Reverend Mueller always prayed and trusted God to provide. The following story illustrates the great faith of Brother Mueller.

"The children are dressed and ready for school.

But there is no food for them to eat," the housemother of the orphanage informed George Mueller. George asked her to take the 300 children into the dining room and have them sit at the tables. He thanked God for the food and waited. George knew God would provide food for the children as he always did. Within minutes, a baker knocked on the door. "Mr. Mueller," he said, "last night I could not sleep. Somehow, I knew that you would need bread this morning. I got up and baked three batches for you. I will bring it in."

Soon, there was another knock at the door. It was the milkman. His cart had broken down in front of the orphanage. The milk would spoil by the time the wheel was fixed. He asked George if he could use some free milk. George smiled as the milkman brought in ten large cans of milk. It was just enough for the 300 thirsty children.[10]

At Shepherd's Arms we tried like George Mueller to share our needs with our Heavenly Father and then trust Him to supply what was needed

---

10 "George Mueller, Orphanages Built by Prayer." *Christianity. com: https://www.christianity.com/church/church-history/ church-history-for-kids/george-mueller-orphanages-built-by-prayer-11634869.html* (February 4, 2020).

and bring it forth at just the right time. We had always tithed or given firstfruits on every gift we received that was not restricted funding. We based this pattern of giving on Proverbs 3:9–10 and Malachi 3:10–12.

One Thursday we were faced with the choice of paying our tithes to the Lord or paying our staff. We chose to honor the Lord with our promise and let Him take care of our staff. When we had finished writing the very last tithe check, our doorbell rang. One of our faithful donors was standing there with a check for several thousand dollars, giving us an offering on the proceeds of her inheritance. That check was just enough to pay our entire staff. The Lord has never been late to meet our needs.

About five years after we founded Shepherd's Arms we were praying for general operating funds, and the Holy Spirit led us to call a gentleman in Bristol, Tennessee, who owned a large pharmaceutical company. When I dialed the number expecting a secretary of this very large company to answer the phone, I was shocked after I asked for the owner. The gentleman who answered was the owner and was temporarily answering the phone for his secretary. I explained to him what we did, and he immediately said he would overnight a check for $9,999 to us because if it were $10,000 it would require a board meeting. We were not troubled by the lack of one dollar but rather thrilled that the Lord had orchestrated this marvelous donation.

Several months later we asked this same gentleman and his foundation for $125,000 and asked for an appointment to meet him. It was a five-hour drive to Bristol from Chattanooga, so we left early that morning. Little did we know that this man's secretary had tried to call us to tell us not to come because the man was home in bed sick. When we arrived five hours later in Bristol, the secretary told us he was not there yet. She did not tell us that she had secretly called him and told him we were there. He immediately got out of bed, dressed, and came to his office. When he walked in, he reached inside his suit pocket and handed us a check for $125,000. Then he put his arms around us and prayed God's blessings on us. In that moment it felt as though God the Father had shown up and embraced us, wrapping us in His eternal arms of love and affirming us that He was and always would be our provider and protector. We left Bristol that day knowing the glory of God had preceded us. A marvelous scripture comes to mind from Deuteronomy 33:27 that promises, "The eternal God is your refuge, And underneath are the everlasting arms."

Soon after that visit I was sitting at the piano one day and the Lord gave me the words and music to a sweet chorus I often sing called "Abba, I Belong to You."

Abba, My Father God,

I belong to You.

Abba, My Daddy God,

I'm your child it's true.

We are family, for eternity,

Oh—Abba, I belong to You.

ABBA, I BELONG TO YOU

Music and lyrics: MARY ANN SANDERS

Andante - Worshipful

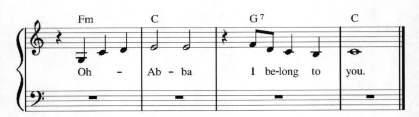

It's a wonderful experience to know the security of belonging to the Heavenly Father. A practice I often engage in is to simply close my eyes and lift my hands to the Lord, saying, "Abba, I belong to You." Sometimes I repeat this process of affirming that Abba is my Daddy God several times until I truly sense His Divine Presence.

Chapter 15

EXPANDING OUR TENT STAKES

"Enlarge the place of your tent, And let them stretch out the curtains of your dwellings; Do not spare; Lengthen your cords, and strengthen your stakes. For you shall expand to the right and to the left, And your descendants will inherit the nations, And make the desolate cities inhabited."

— ISAIAH 54:2-3

As the ministry began to grow, we launched a building campaign in 2001 and asked the Lord to provide $777,000 for Phase One. We wanted to triple the number of homeless residents we could serve. Many local foundations, corporations, churches, and individuals gave funding to underwrite this project, but a surprise gift arrived in the mail one afternoon that was so inspiring. The same man who had taken us in his arms and given us $125,000 had now sent a $400,000 check and a letter from his foundation in Bristol asking us to keep the gift anonymous because he wanted God to get all the glory. What a great policy for giving a gift to the Lord! Give it anonymously so when you get to heaven you will receive a reward publicly.

It took two more years to secure the full $777,000 for Phase One, but the day finally arrived. Then it took two more years to build Phase One. Phase One included acquisition of three more houses that would be torn down to make way for the new dormitory. The Lord never wastes our talents. Jim and I were so glad to be licensed realtors so we could handle all the property acquisition and demolition processes.

Completion of Phase One left us with a brick shell with no interior finishes, including plumbing or electrical. When this new building was complete it would be large enough to house thirty-six residents and feed seventy-five in the dining room.

It was a good thing we didn't know it would take another fourteen years to secure the remaining funds of more than a million dollars we needed to complete Phase Two. We knew we were not to borrow any money, but we were criticized by many in the community saying we didn't have enough faith to borrow money. What they didn't understand was that sometimes it takes more faith to wait on the money rather than going into debt. We could have easily borrowed the money because we had the president of a local bank on our board of directors and collateral to back up the loan, but that wasn't the mandate God had given us to follow. Most importantly, we wanted to obey the Lord and do exactly what He asked us to do.

The waiting rooms in our lives are filled to capacity with God's greatest blessings and fruitful disguises. The problems most of us face consist of running the red lights and rushing through the stop signs God places before us. We often miss God's most excellent choices and detailed fingerprints because of impulsive, hasty decisions. The prayer prayed by a wise, seasoned old Christian gentleman would be an enhancement to our relationship with God: "Lord, slow me down.

I'm going too fast and I'm missing the sound of Your voice."

The fourteen-year wait was a gift from the Lord because so many wonderful things happened during that time—things like housing almost a thousand homeless women and children for four to six months or seeing thirty-five hundred individuals make decisions to follow Jesus at Shepherd's Arms. There are so many wonderful, amazing stories displaying the glory of God during those fourteen years that I want to share some of them with you in the next few pages.

Chapter 16

THE
WHISKEY HOUSE

*"Ask, and it will be given to you; seek, and
you will find; knock, and it will be opened
to you."*

— MATTHEW 7:7

I can still remember the erratic sound of his
intoxicated voice as he begged, "Please, lady,
come inside." My daughter and I were delivering
bread to the neighbors around the mission as Joe
was lurching over the front porch of a run-down
house we had labeled "the whiskey house." This
infamous house was known by all in the hood as a
place where illegal drugs, alcohol, and illicit sex
were distributed.

Shortly after we purchased the mission property, we spent several weeks picking up whiskey bottles along with needles and other unholy paraphernalia (enough to fill more than two hundred lawn bags) that had just been tossed over the newly installed mission fence from the front porch of the whiskey house. Unlike most days, today Joe was not cursing profusely or rolling around on the front porch out of control in a drunken stupor. Something was different today, so I chose to lock my daughter in the car while I went inside at his request.

As I entered through the front door, I caught a glimpse of a frail lady lying on a sofa about four feet away. She was bald, with absolutely no hair. Then I saw the trach tube and asked her, "What's your name?"

She barely whispered, "J-u-d-y" as she held her weak finger over the invasive tube in her throat.

I asked, "Are you a Christian, Judy?"

She replied, "No."

I said, "Well, I just want you to know that Jesus Christ sent me by today to tell you He loves you deeply and cares about you more than you know."

When I said the name *Jesus*, the tears began flowing like a runaway river. A few minutes later Judy accepted Jesus Christ as Lord and Savior. I later discovered that Judy in her younger years had been a convicted murderer and drug dealer, but she had served her time in prison. Now she had received her full pardon through justification by faith in the works of Jesus Christ on the cross of Calvary. The whiskey house had now witnessed one significant salvific event.

Several months later an elderly man named Bob moved into the whiskey house. Bob had become crippled by diabetes and a recent stroke, so my husband made regular visits to the whiskey house to deliver evening meals prepared for Bob at the mission. One evening in March Jim felt a genuine urgency prompted by the Holy Spirit that he must visit Bob. When he arrived he found Bob in a deeply troubled state of mind.

Bob asked Jim to pray, and he too accepted Jesus Christ as Lord. A bonus of physical healing was granted Bob at this important encounter with God.

As my husband started to leave, Bob said, "Jim, I'm so glad you came this evening. Something told me you would be here. All day long I've been sitting here planning to get my pistol and go across the street and shoot her right between the eyes. I planned to kill her, but now I know that was wrong."

You see, Bob's fiancée had broken up with him and he had been responding to the wrong voice, but thank God for His mercy, grace, and gentle voice of unconditional love. The whiskey house was now the setting for a second miraculous happening.

When Shepherd's Arms began the building campaign, acquisition of several key pieces of property was significant. The whiskey house was the most important piece of property needed. We had tried to purchase it for years, but the owners refused to sell it to the mission because they didn't like Christians. We and many of our intercessors began to pray we would be able to purchase the whiskey house because we needed it for the back entrance to the new dormitory. I remember driving by the office of the owners of the whiskey house around seven-thirty one morning after much prayer and multitudes of prayer walks. As I passed by, a stranger walked out of the office and locked the door. I stopped and asked where the former owners were. When I discovered they had sold the property, my heart sank with disappointment.

I asked the gentleman who had purchased the property, and he named the new owner. I just about fell out of my car from shock when I heard the name of one of the ministry's faithful corporate donors. An agreement to purchase the whiskey house was drawn up that same afternoon, and the property was closed out two weeks later. Shepherd's Arms Rescue Mission now owned the whiskey house, and the Lord Jesus Christ had redeemed this land for His glory and honor.

We need to remember our God is faithful. He answers prayer. He always works with purpose and meaning. He is sovereign. We can never out-give Him. Matthew 7:7 declares, "Ask, and it shall be given to you; seek, and you will find; knock, and it will be opened to you."

Chapter 17

CATTLE ON A THOUSAND HILLS

"For every beast of the forest is Mine, And the cattle on a thousand hills."

— PSALM 50:10

The steadfast love of the Lord never ceases. His mercies are new every morning. Great is His faithfulness.

As ministers, Jim and I were not rich in material possessions, but we have a Heavenly Father who is. Our only child, Mary Anna, was able to attend a private all-girls' school for six years that cost as much or more than most private universities to attend. She graduated debt free because of the lavish generosity of our Lord.

I well remember her first day of registration at this elite school and how the Lord had strategically placed His servants waiting around every corner to help. The very group of ladies who had prayed Shepherd's Arms Rescue Mission into existence served as faculty members at this school. When we selected Mary Anna's books at the bookstore and tried to pay for them, we were told they had already been paid for. We quickly discovered that Jane, Betsy, Maria, Peggy, and Nancy had paid for our daughter's books. We were totally ignorant of prep-school fashions, and the Lord even handled that as Jane purchased Mary Anna a very cool and trendy jacket to match her required school uniforms.

God is so faithful. He is never late but rarely early either. His grace is saved for just the right moment to be imparted to make the deepest impact in our lives. Mary Anna did experience a bit of social adjustment the first year since her dad often transported her to school in his old 1977 Chevy truck, which was more than used and extremely weathered. It was common practice for Mary Anna to duck and hide on the floorboard when they would drive past the track team in this antique jalopy. She was more than delighted the second year when we saved enough money to get a paint job for the truck. One paint job and the truck instantly became a classic that resurrected our daughter from the floorboard into full view at the dashboard.

At graduation from the Girls Preparatory School Mary Anna received a presidential scholarship and was able to attend Lee University, where she graduated magna cum laude with no debt. She acquired two degrees while there—a B.S. in biology and a B.A. in English. She had taken a mission trip to Ghana, West Africa, while at Lee and felt the Lord calling her into the medical profession. Her heart's desire was to become a doctor.

The cost of medical school was over a quarter of a million dollars and seemed like a huge mountain to even attempt to climb. First, my husband and I gave her all our retirement funds. Then she received a Timothy Scholarship from the Chattanooga Christian Community Foundation, where individual donors could contribute and receive tax exemption while helping each student. Somehow the Lord had miraculously provided $230,000 and we were so thankful.

Then the last quarter of medical school she was short $20,000. I took a leap of faith and called a gentleman in another city who was known for being very generous. When I asked for the $20,000, he immediately said no. My husband and I were not quitters, so we went into the chapel and got on the floor and prayed to our Provider, asking Him for the $20,000. Here's the exact wording we prayed: "Father, You own the cattle on a thousand hills. Please sell a few head and send us this $20,000. Lord, please explain to John (the man who had said no) how important this is and let him change His mind."

Early the next morning John's secretary called to tell us the Lord had spoken very specifically to him during the night and had told John to share the $20,000 with Mary Anna. Then she said, "John wanted me to tell you to remember this: God still owns the cattle on a thousand hills." We were so encouraged by that exact wording that we had prayed that we shared it with John. He was blessed because God had confirmed His desire with us as well as with John.

Our daughter graduated from medical school completely debt free. Her firstfruits of service when she graduated from residency were to go to Nepal and climb the Himalayas to minister God's grace to women and children who had never heard the name of Jesus Christ. She taught the women in the villages how to deliver babies. During her tenure in Nepal she visited nine rescue houses where sexually trafficked women needed medical attention, which she lovingly gave them.

After residency and specialist training, Mary Anna opened her own medical office in Chattanooga. The name of her practice is "Fearfully and Wonderfully Made OB/GYN," from Psalm 139.

The Lord is the banker of the universe, and He is not bankrupt. He so enjoys helping His children as they join Him in the work He is doing. After all, He owns the cattle on a thousand hills and He also owns the hills. "The earth is the Lord's, and all its fullness, The world and those who dwell therein" (Psalm 24:1).

Chapter 18

SINGING OVER BARRENNESS

*"Sing, O barren, You who have not borne!
Break forth into singing, and cry aloud,
You who have not labored with child! For
more are the children of the desolate Than
the children of the married woman," says
the Lord.*

—ISAIAH 54:1

In my lifetime I have experienced many areas of barrenness—spiritually, mentally, emotionally, relationally, and financially. Discovering the blessings found in Isaiah 54:1 brought much enrichment to my life. The power of this was driven home pragmatically just recently as our elective annual audit was being conducted at

Shepherd's Arms. Our auditor, Sherri, had been married for a number of years and truly wanted to have a child. She and her husband had visited multiple doctors and had been told pregnancy was not medically possible.

Sherri asked me to pray that she would be able to conceive a child even though man had told her it was impossible. I did pray for her, but I also shared with her that Isaiah 54:1 instructs those who are barren to sing over their barrenness. I suggested she might want to go home and begin to sing the Word of God over her desired nursery. Sherri latched on to God's Word in faith and she did indeed go home and began singing God's Word over the situation.

The weeks and months went by and I had not spoken to Sherri since the last audit. One day before our next audit I called her about an issue we needed help with, and she said she wasn't feeling great that day. I told her I was so sorry and would be praying for her. She immediately replied, "You don't know yet, do you?"

I told her I didn't know what she was talking about. "I'm pregnant and this is just morning sickness," she said. I was so excited that I just had to ask her if she had been singing over the situation. Absolutely, she had been.

By the time our next audit was due she had delivered a healthy, precious baby boy. He was perfect in every way. Sherri was so happy and blessed to be the mother of such a fine baby boy. To God be all the glory! Great things He does through His Word, which is alive and very active and sharp.

Our music minister at Shepherd's Arms had a daughter-in-law who was experiencing the same kind of problems. She also began to sing over the nursery, and since that time two precious children have been birthed through her. Our daughter, who is an ob-gyn, has shared Isaiah 54:1 with several of her patients who were having difficulty, and she has had the joy of delivering sweet healthy babies to these loving mothers. The Lord watches over His Word to perform it.

The purpose of this testimony is not to give a formula to use in every situation but only to share how God has worked miraculously in the past. He always works individually with each of His children. Matthew 19:26 shouts volumes of truth as Jesus says, "With men this is impossible, but with God all things are possible."

Maybe your barrenness is in another area, or perhaps your faith is waning because of lost loved ones. There is no greater area to sing God's Word over than barren spiritual ground. My experience of singing God's Word over lost loved ones has been extremely productive because it always boosts and encourages our faith. Psalm 96:1 exhorts and invites us to "sing to the Lord a new song! Sing to the Lord, all the earth."

What area of barrenness is God calling you to sing over today?

Chapter 19

A LITTLE CHILD
SHALL LEAD THEM

"And a little child shall lead them."

—ISAIAH 11:6

Twenty-two years ago Shepherd's Arms Rescue Mission orchestrated a summer youth camp for at-risk inner-city youth. During that time frame two very brilliant and precocious young Hispanic boys named Javier and Oscar brightened the camp. They never missed an after-school tutoring class or a summer youth enrichment day camp. Both young boys accepted Jesus Christ as Lord early on at Shepherd's Arms and demonstrated their great love by obeying the Lord in every way. Their family was from Mexico.

The mother spoke perfect English and Spanish, but the father was still learning the English language. Maria, the mother, was faithful to make sure Javier and Oscar were always on time and ready to study.

Week after week for years we invited the mother to attend our Sunday afternoon chapel services at four o'clock. She was always very polite and respectful and said she would come but never showed up. After two and a half long years of invitations and no-shows, she finally came to chapel and brought her three children. Almost immediately after the Word of God was shared in the service, she accepted Jesus as her Lord. A month later we looked out the mission window on a Sunday afternoon and saw Maria, her three sons, and her husband Cesar coming up the walkway. She had encouraged her husband to come to the service, where he too accepted Jesus as his Lord and Savior.

I was really interested in knowing why after all this time Maria had decided to attend the service, so I asked her. She told me that for two years she had watched Javier and Oscar come home so excited about this Jesus. They memorized scripture, they asked her to read stories to them from the Bible, and they couldn't wait to get back to the mission to study more of God's Word. Maria told me she became jealous and wanted to know how to find the kind of joy and happiness her sons enjoyed. Javier and Oscar had been the light that shined in the darkness to help bring their mother into the kingdom of God. Naturally, the father saw this same kind of peace and joy and he too wanted to experience it.

Javier and Oscar had made their mother hunger and thirst for righteousness. Someone is always watching us and observing the way we live our lives. Hopefully our lives make the world around us hunger and thirst for righteousness. Hopefully we are the bright lights that shine for Jesus in a very dark and desperate world.

Matthew 5:16 instructs us to "let your light so shine before men, that they may see your good works and glorify your Father in heaven."

Chapter 20

SOMEONE IS ALWAYS WATCHING

Meanwhile, live in such a way that you are a credit to the Message of Christ.
— PHILIPPIANS 1:27 MSG

Several months ago my family and I were eating in a Chinese restaurant in Tiftonia, Tennessee. The twenty-five-year-old Chinese server waited until we were leaving to tell us that when we ate there it always made him feel happy. I immediately told this young man that the reason for the happiness and joy was Jesus Christ is the Lord of our lives.

The next time we ate at this restaurant, Peter, the young server, asked us if we would teach him about our God. For the next few months, once a week our family would take Peter out to dinner and share the message of Jesus with him. We presented Peter with a Chinese/English Bible, and soon after, he accepted Jesus as his Lord and Savior. Peter attended chapel services many months at Shepherd's Arms. A few summers ago he served as a camp counselor at Shepherd's Arms in summer youth camp for homeless children. During this summer camp Peter led many young people in accepting Jesus as Lord. Peter is also a witness to his mother, father, and sister, who still live in China.

The simple truth is this: God has called us all to be His ambassadors. Wherever we go, whatever we do, whatever we say, we can be confident that someone is watching us and listening to what we have to say. The scriptural challenge comes to us from Philippians 1:27 as it mandates, "Meanwhile, live in such a way that you are a credit to the Message of Christ" (MSG).

Chapter 21

MAN, THIS IS HEAVEN!

"In my Father's house are many mansions; if it were not so, I would have told you. I go to prepare a place for you."

— JOHN 14:2

When Jim and I joined the Lord Jesus Christ in the work He was doing among homeless women and children, widows, and at-risk inner-city youth, we failed to include men in our oikos, or worldview of ministry. Thank God, He had no intentions for us to exclude men from our model, so He has delicately and intricately woven into the fabric of our work with Him an occasional ministry to men.

Jim shares the following story about Sam.

His frail, thin, dark-skinned frame was seen daily on the streets of Alton Park, South Chattanooga, always pushing a grocery cart as he rummaged through garbage containers for food, clothing, shoes, and so on. We came to know him as Sam, an elderly former construction worker, who now wandered aimlessly every day searching for real meaning in his life. He gathered aluminum cans to recycle and on the first of the month he received a small Social Security check with which he usually bought a few bottles of wine. He and his friends on the corner below the mission drank themselves into a stupor.

We urged him to come to our chapel service on Sunday afternoon, and one day he surprised us all by showing up. Sam surrendered his life to the Lord Jesus. He shared many intimate details of his life with us. Sam had served our country in active combat as a young man and understood the fact that the Lord had protected his life and brought him safely back home. He routinely shared about his experiences in the Battle of Pork Chop Hill in the Korean War. Sam's combat experiences had left him with many troubled emotions he was trying to overcome with God's help.

Sam shared with us that he lived in an abandoned house in Alton Park. The house had no running water or electricity, but it provided a makeshift roof over his head. He had found an old junky kerosene heater he used to stay warm in the winter. We provided the kerosene for him. One day he came to the mission very upset because he had been evicted from this old house and he had no place to call home.

My wife and I asked him what he thought about permanent housing in a place for the elderly. He wasn't really sure he wanted that, but he agreed to go there with me to look the place over. Sam and I met with the authorities, and they qualified him for a government apartment in this high-rise for the elderly. When the manager took us on a tour to view the apartment, we saw it had a lovely view of Lookout Mountain and of South Chattanooga, Sam's old stomping grounds. When I asked Sam what he thought about the apartment, he instantly replied, "Man, this is heaven!" Our guide asked him to repeat what he had said, and again Sam said, "Man, this is heaven! Sure, I will take it."

For approximately six years Sam continued to live in that apartment, never missing a rent payment. He regularly attended our chapel services and offered his ministry gifts as a faithful, committed volunteer. He served as our bus captain and rode on the mission bus every Sunday, assisting everyone in getting on and off the bus safely.

Sam truly loved Jesus Christ and he was compulsive about keeping all his biblical notes in a special case where he could rehearse them over and over. Once in a small-group meeting Sam was truly open to the Holy Spirit of the Lord as he shared with us how the Lord had helped him understand that his life had always been in God's hands. Sam knew the only reason he was still here on earth was because God had not finished his plan for his life.

As Sam left the mission van after the small-group meeting that night he said, "You just can't hide from God. He sees and knows all about our lives. From now on I am going to let God run my life full-speed ahead."

Several hours later the police rang the doorbell of the mission and asked us to identify Sam's personal belongings. Sam had been involved in a fatal accident —he had been run over by a truck and killed. God had graciously called Sam home.

My wife and I spoke at Sam's military funeral, where he received full honors as a cherished veteran. As I reflect upon his home going, I can only imagine Sam's wondrous expression and exclamation as he was ushered into his heavenly home that Jesus had prepared for him. And I can hear Sam saying to Jesus, "Yes, this really *is* heaven!"

Chapter 22

THE DANCE
OF VICTORY

But thanks be to God, who gives us the
victory through our Lord Jesus Christ.
— 1 CORINTHIANS 15:57

The grimace on her face was a mere reflection of the deep rejection, shame, and punishment her dysfunctional family had labeled to her soul. Nineteen years can seem like an eternity if you are a victim of daily neglect, abandonment, and abuse. Jane was a senior in high school when she and her five-month-old daughter entered the mission as residential clients. She was a victim of rape. Her mother blamed her for being victimized and consequently kicked her out of the family. It would seem that life was already difficult enough, but on top of everything else Jane was a special education student and mentally challenged.

Bitterness, rage, fear, and hopelessness described Jane as she began her spiritual journey at Shepherd's Arms Rescue Mission. She was furious with God, her rapist, family, teachers, and anyone else she met on the street. Jane wanted nothing to do with a God who allowed all these bad things to happen to her. For several weeks Jane sat in chapel services with her head down, trying to ignore what was being taught from the Bible. The first three weeks Jane was in residence she did not speak many words to anyone at the mission.

Easter Sunday was rapidly approaching, and Shepherd's Arms scheduled a special showing of the movie *The Passion of the Christ*. After the movie Jane had a different countenance and the mission staff soon discovered that her joy was linked to the fact that she had given her heart to the Lord Jesus Christ.

The spiritual lights began to glow for Jane. Her eyes became filled with a renewed sense of hope, and she was experiencing real peace of mind for the first time in her life. She was learning exactly what these words in Romans 8:1 mean: "There is therefore now no condemnation to those who are in Christ Jesus." Condemnation had been her constant companion until Jesus Christ became her valued partner and friend who would stick closer than a brother. The music of Jane's life was picking up momentum.

Several months passed and one evening Jane came into the mission office and barely mumbled the words "I need a dress." "Why do you need a dress, Jane?" She replied, "I want to go to the prom." I asked her with whom and she replied, "I want to go by myself."

I asked her if she would like my daughter to take her shopping and, of course, she agreed. My daughter was twenty-one years old at the time and she took Jane shopping and to dinner several times. Words cannot express the sheer joy and excitement that filled everyone's heart at the mission as Jane came back from one of those shopping trips and modeled her lovely pastel pink prom dress and clear dancing shoes that looked like the ones Cinderella had worn to the ball. Jane's self-esteem soared like an eagle flying over the Grand Canyon as everyone at the mission complimented her and expressed a sincere belief in her.

Every victim who has been forced to dance with the devil in defeat needs to experience the joy of going to a senior prom with Jesus Christ as the escort. Jane no longer danced the dance of defeat because Jesus was her new partner—and they dance the dance of victory!

Chapter 23

BEER TRUCK CRASHES INTO CHRIST

"With men this is impossible, but with God all things are possible."

— MATTHEW 19:26

The smell of his breath was one hundred percent proof that alcohol had become his taskmaster. The guys in the hood always joked about him stealing beer off the beer truck while the driver was busy unloading the beverages. In six years I had never seen this man sober. Even though he was only forty years old, the doctors had told Leroy he was going to die if he didn't quit drinking alcohol and doing drugs.

Leroy stood on the front porch of the mission and conveyed this message of doom from the doctors. I had personally shared Christ and witnessed to Leroy many times and given him food and drink, but nothing seemed to penetrate his hard, cold, inebriated soul. The mission staff added Leroy to the prayer list of those in need of salvation.

Months and years passed, and Leroy continued to drink excessively and use illegal drugs. Then one day we heard the news from Leroy's mother that he was terminally ill with cancer. My husband prayed with Leroy's mother for his healing even though the doctors said nothing more could be done medically. Leroy's mother begged the physicians to operate. Finally they did but warned the family that Leroy probably would not make it through the surgery.

That was fourteen years ago and today Leroy is cancer free, strong in his faith in the Lord Jesus Christ, and working at Shepherd's Arms Rescue Mission as a deliveryman. He no longer steals beer off the beer truck, but he does ride in the Shepherd's Arms Ministry truck and delivers food to needy families.

Does God still do miracles of healing? Absolutely! Did he heal Leroy of what the doctors labeled as terminal cancer? Yes, indeed! Can God use broken vessels in His service to glorify His name? Without a doubt!

In my finite mind I had given up on Leroy by labeling him a hopeless case. The Lord delights in doing the impossible, the least likely, the unexpected God-sized feats that only God can do.

Perhaps you have a Leroy in your own family. My challenge for you is to present your impossible situation to the Lord Jesus Christ and then be prepared to see a miracle. The Bible is very clear as the message of Matthew 19:26 comes crashing through, saying, "With men this is impossible, but with God all things are possible."

Chapter 24

BLOWING THE DARK CLOUDS AWAY

*And don't allow yourselves to be weary
or disheartened in planting good seeds,
for the season of reaping the wonderful
harvest you've planted is coming!*

—GALATIANS 6:9 TPT

It was one of those rare but very real overcast dreary days when the sun was hiding behind dark, ominous clouds, physically and spiritually. This had been a week when no one wanted to obey the rules of the shelter. Everyone was ungrateful and flaunting the badge of entitlement. The phone and doorbell rang non-stop with more folks needing help than we had room or resources to offer. When resources are low and requests for assistance are high, it is very challenging.

I was physically, mentally, and spiritually exhausted. I was struggling with the slow speed of transformation with the population of homeless women and children we served. You could say I was wrestling with the Lord over a scripture in James 1:4 where it says to let patience have her perfect work so you will be complete, perfect, and lacking nothing. It was obvious I was lacking patience and encouragement. James 1:2 says to "count it all joy when you fall into various trials."

That afternoon I decided time was not my friend after twenty-three years of helping folks over the hurdles of life. I found myself weary in well-doing. As mentioned earlier, sometimes as Christians we forget that life doesn't always circulate around the ceiling.

When the doorbell rang very late in the day, I slumped back in my chair, dreading to hear another request we might not be able to meet. But I reluctantly pulled myself up by the bootstraps and headed to the door, expecting the worst. Much to my delight, when I opened the door I saw a young, handsome, very well-groomed African-American man in his early twenties smiling from ear to ear. He told me his name and asked if his church could adopt some of our children for Christmas.

I was instantly refreshed and gained my second spiritual wind as I realized that he was a giver and not someone needing help. When he sat down to talk with me and Jim, he said, "I just want to thank you for helping me and my mother when I was seven years old. We were homeless and had no place to live and you took us in and helped us get back on our feet." He said he was now a teacher and was working on his master's degree. He spent his spare time mentoring young Black men who had lost their way. He said he just wanted to give back to the people who had helped his family.

My husband and I spent over an hour visiting with this young man and listening to his inspiring story. It had been fifteen years since he had been a resident at Shepherd's Arms, but he never forgot the love of God he had received. When Christmas rolled around, he rang our doorbell again bringing bicycles, toy trucks, dolls, and many other gifts for homeless children.

Approximately one week later around nine in the evening I left the mission and stopped at a nearby gas station to fill up my car. Just as I was about to open my gas tank, I saw a young African-American man running full speed across the parking lot toward me like a freight train. I was initially startled until he came closer and threw his arms around me and hugged me. I recognized him as a former student in our after-school program at the mission. He was so excited to see me, and I was so relieved to discover I knew him. He said he just wanted to thank everyone at Shepherd's Arms for teaching him respect and good manners. He said it had helped him make a lot of progress in life. He was so proud to report that he was a freshman in college and doing well. He had a good job.

He had grown up in a family of eight living in a public housing project. Now he proudly said he had his own place out of the projects. All the credit was given to the Lord Jesus. He just kept thanking us for being there when he had needed direction and encouragement. I had not seen this young man in seven years, yet God had ordained this moment to encourage us in His work.

The Holy Spirit used both these young men to blow the dark clouds of weariness and discouragement away so the Sonshine of Jesus could break through and renew the vision of our calling. Only Jesus can bring hope to the hopeless, faith to the fearful, joy to the brokenhearted, strength to the weak, and refreshment to those who are weary. The Word of God in Galatians 6:9 reminds us of this great truth: "And let us not grow weary while doing good, for in due season we shall reap if we do not lose heart."

Just seeing the zeal and contentment in the eyes of those two young men was a magnificent reward to receive as confirmation that we were indeed joining the Lord in the work He was doing.

Chapter 25

LISA'S TRIBUTE

For I am not ashamed of the gospel of Christ: for it is the power of God unto salvation to everyone that believes, to the Jew first, and also to the Greek.

— ROMANS 1:16

The great honor of serving a multitude of diverse individuals has been the joy of joining Jesus in His great work among homeless women and children, widows, and at-risk inner-city youth. His mercies are new every morning, and it is so very exciting to see what His omnipotent hand reveals. Our daughter, Dr. Mary Anna Sanders, ministers as a biblical educator at

Shepherd's Arms Ministry. She shares the following story about Lisa.

My neighborhood (Alton Park) is quiet on most days—full of chirping birds, scrambling chipmunks, and children laughing in the distance. You know, the way I have described it sounds basically like a Disney fairytale. Occasionally a driver blasts their car's rever-berating bass subwoofer, or the shrill sirens from the fire department down the street will tip the balance of peaceful quiet to outright noisy. Minimal to rare, however, are the overt and obvious sounds of gunshots and violence—though it is what my neighborhood is known for in our local media. This doesn't mean the spiritual oppression within the homes here is not pervasive. It certainly does not mean that children never go to bed hungry or abused. However, I would like to dispel the myth that it is the gun-and-knives club our local news makes it out to be.

On May 5, 2018, however, there was a new sound in my hood. I was standing in the newly completed dorm quietly preparing to play Lisa's favorite Bible study song on my guitar when I first heard the rumble. When I stood to see what was going on, I could visualize the pack of motorcycles coming up from 38th street, stretching down Alton Park Boulevard and up West Avenue into our new back driveway. The entire length of the way. They were coming here. To Lisa's memorial service. My mind was blown as biker by biker double-parked the length of the long driveway in the back. Leather vests and chaps, visible weapons, and quite frankly paraphernalia that I have no idea what it was for (chains with balls and spikes, for example) adorned most of these bikers. More skin was covered in tattoos than was bare. Not representative of a single race but all, one by one the bikers came in until we had the largest crowd of unchurched folk that Shepherd's Arms has ever seen . . . or maybe that I have ever seen anywhere I've ever been in the world in a single setting.

You see, we had lost Lisa—one of our dearly beloved sisters in our Saturday Bible study—but heaven had gained another saint. She was truly an example of a life literally transformed by the gospel because Jesus really does change everything. She was famous for answering my "How are ya this morning?" question with something like "I woke up this side of the dirt, so I know it's gonna be another good day" or "I'm healed" or any number of true, uplifting statements. She had fought her battle with metastatic lung cancer FAITHFULLY and BRAVELY as a girl with a Sword just living her daily life without rival and not allowing that old devil to steal her joy. She was the mother of two young men and friend to many in our ministry and also in the building where she lived. However, unknown to me was the widespread nature of her reputation. This little lady, who would be viewed as small in the world's eyes, had a *great* mission field around her, larger than any I have known.

Crammed into the great room, we proceeded with the memorial service planned for our dear friend, which included a presentation of the Good News and Mom's and my rendition of Lisa's favorite Saturday Bible study song—Crowder's

"All My Hope."[11] You may be thinking that sounds benign enough, but I will admit that second verse that says "I'm no stranger to the prison, I've worn shackles and chains" took on a bigger-than-life meaning that day, and I was perhaps praying full time to keep from shaking in my boots. I'm not certain I wasn't visibly shaking despite all the prayer.

After the service while we were serving lunch, a man with a teardrop tattoo under his eye (just the outline, not completely shaded in; I understand this may only mean attempted murder) kept asking *me specifically* for more and more banana pudding. He kept getting refills. Usually I am a stickler for the rules, but much was at stake on this day, and I may have been feeling under-armed since I had left my Smith and Wesson back home across the street. Kidding aside, fighting the spiritual battle in that room was full-out war. Several of the bikers got up and left as the crux of the gospel story was being told. The last

11 David Crowder and Ed Cash, "All My Hope," ©WorshipArtistry.com.

time I felt that kind of spiritual oppression, I was trying to sleep in my bug bivvy in a tiny one-room home that hung on the side of the Himalayas while a little Nepali girl screamed with night terrors. I felt the weight of this opportunity at Lisa's memorial service heavily, realizing that this could be the greatest and maybe even perhaps the only opportunity to share the love of Christ with the people there. Eternity could be literally hanging in the balance.

In the morning prior to Lisa's memorial service, we had been studying in our Beth Moore study *James: Mercy Triumphs* how faith and favoritism don't mix. These powerful words are from the second chapter of James:

> *My brothers, do not show favoritism as you hold on to the faith in our glorious Lord Jesus Christ. For example, a man comes into your meeting wearing a gold ring and dressed in fine clothes, and a poor man dressed in dirty clothes also comes in. If you look with favor on the man wearing the fine clothes and say, "Sit here in a good place," and yet you say to the poor man, "Stand over there," or "Sit*

here on the floor by my footstool," haven't you discriminated among yourselves and become judges with evil thoughts? Listen, my dear brothers: Didn't God choose the poor in this world to be rich in faith and heirs of the kingdom that He has promised to those who love Him?

—JAMES 2:1–5 HCSB

As I looked around the jam-packed area, examining the variety of folks mixed together in that very new and nice room, it was apparent that the only thing shared in common was the love and respect for the life of our dear friend, Lisa. And it was the love of Christ in Lisa that had attracted such a variety of people to her. In Luke 5:32 Jesus says, "I have come not to call the 'righteous,' but to call those who fail to measure up and bring them to repentance" (TPT). A white girl from rural Georgia with biracial children, Lisa had a plethora of life experience—including some very negative experiences with "the church." Instead of allowing those things in her past to make her bitter, she followed the gospel message of Jesus and allowed her life to be a light before men (Matthew 5:16). What greater testimony truly could one have?

So I asked myself, *What kind of crowd will I attract at my memorial service?* Lisa hung out with those with whom Jesus would have hung, and her impact on their lives and quite possibly their eternity is of infinite value. So I will ask you the same question in closing—what kind of crowd will you attract at your memorial service?

Chapter 26

FATHER, MAY I?

"Examine your motives to make sure you're not showing off when you do your good deeds, only to be admired by others; otherwise, you will lose the reward of your heavenly Father. So when you give to the poor, don't announce it and make a show of it just to be seen by people, like the hypocrites in the streets and in the marketplace. They've already received their reward! But when you demonstrate generosity, do it with pure motives and without drawing attention to yourself. Give secretly and your Father, who sees all you do, will reward you openly."

— MATTHEW 6:1–4 TPT

When we were kids we used to play a super-duper fun game called "Mother, May I?" For hours we would take turns playing the mother asking permission to engage in activities such as taking one step forward or jumping up or turning around or doing whatever the mother in charge gave permission to do. Always we had to preface our request to mother with these words: "Mother, may I?"

Here at Shepherd's Arms during the past twenty-five years we've prefaced all our activities, expansions, and requests with this phrase: "Father, may I?" We would wait for His response because we were taught by Henry Blackaby in his book on experiencing God[12] that we are to always join the Lord in the work He is doing rather than depending on the Lord to join us in the work *we* want to do.

Christmas adoption at Shepherd's Arms Rescue Mission brought the best of God's generous givers together. The sheer joy of purchasing gifts for a homeless mom and her children was unspeakable and full of glory for every participant. The past twenty-plus years we've observed donor after donor give to the Lord. Take my word that there are joyful, hilarious givers and there are Ebenezer Scrooge types that clutch every dime—it would

---

12 Blackaby and King, *Experiencing God: Knowing and Doing the Will of God.*

take the impact of the Jaws of Life to pry them loose from their mammon.

The most amusing and very sad givers are those who publicly advertise as being philanthropists. When and if we received a gift from one of these self-labeled philanthropists, it reminded me of going to the dentist and having an impacted tooth extracted. It's painful, odious, and regretful. By the time you jump through all their man-made hoops, there's no trace of the Lord to be found and the residue is a sense of guilt for having received the funds. Then after they reluctantly give your organization the gift, they want to micromanage every penny of it. On the polarized side you find the gracious, generous, joyful, exuberant givers who can't wait to release their gifts to the Lord and gain tremendous pleasure from the sheer joy of giving.

Over twenty years ago we became acquainted with a family who practiced secret service, over-the-top, lavish giving to the Lord. This family began by adopting several of our homeless families for Christmas. As this relationship deepened, the giving span widened supernaturally. I remember the first time this family adopted at Christmas, they all arrived in a pickup truck loaded to overflowing with beautifully wrapped lavish gifts. We will call this family the "May I" family because every time we had a serious pressing need it seemed that God picked up His proverbial red telephone and called them. In response, they would mail a check for unbelievable amounts of money to cover whatever the need was. Please understand that we didn't call this family and ask them to give; the Holy Spirit supernaturally initiated all the giving. It was not unusual to receive checks for $10,000, $20,000, $30,000, $40,000, $50,000, $60,000, $70,000, and on up the chain of zeros from the "May I" family.

We have cried so many wonderful tears of joy because of the obedience of the "May I" family and their non-assuming, humble generosity. These precious loved ones never requested or expected to get their name in lights or to receive any earthly recognition because they had only one agenda—to glorify the Lord Jesus Christ and bring Him great pleasure.

Normally this family just mailed us a check, but recently one of their children blessed our socks off by sending a $10,000 gift via the Internet through PayPal. This really was the icing on the cake because the entire family had just dropped off checks on one occasion totaling $90,000. It was a merry Christmas and happy new year indeed to the hundreds of needy moms, children, and widows we served.

Whenever we have a serious need and wonder if the Lord wants us to take care of a particular need, we just pray, "Father, may I" and usually the "May I" family gets the memo first and responds immediately. Sadly, the patriarch of this precious family graduated to heaven. Several weeks after his homegoing the ministry was in need of financial assistance. We never told anyone except our Heavenly Father, but almost immediately after our prayer we received a huge check for the exact amount needed to cover the bills. Some unexpected insurance bills arrived right after that and again there was a tremendous need. We prayed again and that same sweet daughter who had e-mailed $10,000 via Pal Pay sent a huge gift in memory of her father.

Praise the Lord for His chosen vessels who are tuned in to the frequency of the Holy Spirit and obey His commands. May I take this opportunity to thank the Lord Jesus Christ and the "May I" family for never being late in caring for His lambs. We are eternally grateful. Thank you for giving to the Lord.

Chapter 27

THE HILLS ARE ALIVE WITH THE SOUND OF GOD'S PROLIFIC MUSIC

"Your God is present among you, a strong Warrior there to save you. Happy to have you back, he'll calm you with his love and delight you with his songs."

— ZEPHANIAH 3:17 MSG

Several years after Shepherd's Arms was up and running, we prayed about a ministry event that would be a fundraiser but most of all a ministry tool. The Lord impressed upon our hearts to have a symphony concert with the featured artist being my dear friend from college Rebecca Cook-Carter. You remember her, don't you? She was the extremely gifted soprano with a Pentecostal preacher for a father.

The problem was that I hadn't seen her or heard from her in over twenty-five years. I called her mother and asked where she was and found out she was with her husband in Germany, teaching and performing. I discovered that before she had left for Germany she had performed regularly with the San Francisco Opera. Her mother gave me her mailing address. While I was preparing to write her, the Holy Spirit spoke to me, telling me to share with her a prayer for her and her family, put it on a cassette tape, and enclose it in the letter.

Approximately two weeks after mailing her the letter, I received a phone call from Becky in Germany. She was crying profusely and totally overwhelmed by the Holy Spirit. She said on the afternoon she received my letter and the tape of me praying for her family, she was in the midst of a huge argument with her husband and was planning to leave him. The Lord had spoken to her through the letter and prayer, advising her to hang in there and work things out with her husband.

Becky was eternally grateful for the prayer and word from the Lord Jesus. She quickly agreed to do the concert with the Chattanooga Symphony. We worked together with the Lord in planning the event and came up with the name of the concert finally as *An Evening to Touch the Heart.*

The anxiety I experienced was significant since I had never planned a symphony concert and there were so many aspects of an event like that to consider. Selection of music, contracting the symphony, selecting the proper venue, advertising the event, acquisition of underwriting expenses, production of videos and coordination of volunteers for the event all seemed gigantic tasks for a rookie. The one variable I kept forgetting was that this was the Lord's concert, not mine, and when He is involved things go impeccably well. The Lord just took control of His concert and made everything fit perfectly like a hand in a glove.

The selected repertoire ranged from very classical selections like the aria "Pace, Pace, Mio, Dio," by Giuseppe Verdi, to more informal medleys of beloved hymns like "Great Is Thy Faithfulness." All the music was easily selected. The night of the rehearsal finally arrived. As I was sitting in the balcony setting up a projector for the volunteer segment with Mary Anna and Jim, I heard the voice of the Holy Spirit whisper in my spirit a message just for me. Don't freak out—it wasn't an audible voice but simply a strong impression I heard. What did He say to me? He whispered to me that the next selection the symphony was going to play was being played just for me. When I looked down at the printed program, I realized the next selection was a medley of songs from *The Sound of Music*. Only the Lord would have known how special and cherished that music was to me. I have loved that music since I was a child because it represented one of the only times my mama and daddy had taken me to a movie as a family unit and we actually enjoyed peaceful, meaningful interaction, which brought great joy to my heart. I wanted to freeze that moment in history because it meant so much to me.

When the maestro picked up his baton to conduct this piece and the music began, it was as though God Himself were conducting that heavenly music. It swept over my soul with a compassionate, loving touch from my Heavenly Father, and it was profound in meaning. The hills truly were alive with the sound of my Heavenly Father's very prolific music in my heart. The Lord always knows how to reward His children with special, unique blessings designed to meet the deepest needs of their lives.

Chapter 28

DON'T SIT ON
THE SOFA

"Cleanliness is, indeed, next to godliness."
— JOHN WESLEY[13]

The past twenty-five years at Shepherd's Arms we've watched hundreds of volunteers come in like a tsunami, volunteer one or two weeks, and then disappear like a whirlwind. When the Lord sends His people, they come in ever so slowly and dip their little toes in to test the waters before easing into the deep end of the ocean. This was the case with Tucker, our volunteer social worker for thirteen years. She came to us from the Lookout Mountain Presbyterian Church and just wanted to offer her services to the Lord Jesus Christ.

Tucker was a gift of the Lord to this mission. At the time she arrived we had no money to pay a social worker. Even if we had had the money, we could never have hired anyone better than Tucker. She was a volunteer "par excellence." During her thirteen-year tenure she helped hundreds of homeless moms and children find the Lord Jesus Christ and their places in life.

Let's just take a short rabbit trail right here as a reminder to affirm that I do not like germs or dirty places. The Lord has a huge sense of humor. That's why, as noted earlier, my first ministry assignment was in a women's prison, the next assignment in three hospitals as a chaplain with one hospital being for children, and now He had placed me in a homeless shelter for women and children. Can you see the progression of germs following me?

While training to be a hospital chaplain we were required to read a book entitled *Don't Sit on the Bed.*[14] Well, that was no problem for me because I was always ministering from a distance—as close to the door as possible.

---

14 William G. Justice, *Don't Sit on the Bed* (Nashville: Broadman Press, 1973).

Now our sweet social worker, Mrs. Tucker, always wanted to do a home visit after our clients moved into permanent housing. I preferred phone calls, but one afternoon she invited me to join her for a site visit. I agreed to go on one condition. You guessed it, didn't you? We would not sit down on the cloth sofa. I suppose my hospital chaplain days had carried over and wisely so.

When we arrived at the home of our former resident, her very precious and sweet mentally challenged child invited us to come inside and asked us to sit down and wait for the mother. I felt just fine standing but I saw Tucker's eyes gazing at the sofa, so my anxiety started to escalate. Inside my body my spirit was shouting, "No, Tucker— don't sit down." About that time Tucker looked at me and said, "Let's sit down, Mary Ann."

Oh, my goodness gracious, Tucker. Really? She sat down and so did I. No sooner had we perched on the sofa than we felt a very warm liquid penetrate and ooze through the backs of our pants. What could this be? Well, it had an odor like a baby's wet diaper, so I assume it must have been something in that category. Holy cow—someone had actually wet the sofa we were sitting on! At that exact instant I wanted to run get my hospital book *Don't Sit on the Bed* and add an addendum titled "And by all means never ever sit on the sofa."

Tucker and I looked at each other. We managed to keep straight faces as we calmly visited with the mother of the family. Of course, my mind was already racing ahead, thinking how fast I could get to a shower and wondering how to protect my car seat on the journey home. I wondered if we would get arrested if we took off our pants and drove home dressed like the Blue Bunny Ice Cream commercial suggests, "Bye, Bye, britches." Simultaneously at that particular moment I was silently shouting "Amen!" to John Wesley's 1791 sermon phrase "Cleanliness is, indeed, next to godliness."

In the car on the way home it was all I could do not to say, "Hey, Tucker—next time let's not sit on the sofa!"

Chapter 29

A MERRY HEART DOES GOOD
LIKE A MEDICINE

A merry heart does good, like medicine,
But a broken spirit dries the bones.

— PROVERBS 17:22

His laughter was more than genuine, and she had compassion, mercy, and love just radiating from every part of her being. The Lord had truly graced us with the cream of the crop when He chose our new house parents to manage the new dormitory expansion. Finding new house parents for a shelter for homeless women and children isn't the easiest task. One has to be literally called to this work to be able to endure.

Terry was my maternal first cousin and his wife, Donna, was the perfect helpmate for Terry as they both gave up a prosperous business to join the Lord in the work He was doing among homeless women and children, widows, and at-risk inner-city youth. We had never had a husband-and-wife team serving in this capacity, but this arrangement was more than perfect in every way. Donna and Terry had no biological children so every child who entered the doors of Shepherd's Arms instantly became family to them.

Caring for more than ten thousand square feet of building plus managing a whole house full of homeless women and children was challenging, to say the least. Every day when I arrived at the shelter, it was spic-and-span clean—there were no exceptions. The floors were polished, the bookshelves were dust free, the kitchen was spotless, all the resident and staff rooms were impeccably clean.

Every morning and afternoon they rotated cleaning different sections of the building, taking great pleasure in caring for the house of the Lord. We never had to suggest that something needed to be cleaned or maintained. Terry and Donna had owned a cleaning business for many years and now they were cleaning with the Lord at His house. They acted like it and enjoyed it.

Their cleaning expertise was most appreciated when our very first family arrived in the new dormitory. The mother of these two beautiful children didn't like our boundaries and failed to abide by our curfew. When we gave her a written warning, she exploded and decided to leave the mission. Unfortunately, she decided to urinate on the new sofa in her dorm room before leaving. Gratitude seems to be antiquated with some people. Donna and Terry immediately knew exactly what to do to clean this new sofa so it was like new.

The most precious gift Terry and Donna delivered to this mission was joy unspeakable and full of glory. This house was instantly filled with laughter and buckets of joy. If they weren't laughing and praising Jesus, they were both interceding in prayer for the Lord's will to be done and His kingdom to come at Shepherd's Arms. It was such a pleasure and encouragement to be around them.

Every mother and child living at the mission sang

the praises of Mr. Terry and Mrs. Donna. The number of new converts increased significantly after their arrival. The morale of all staff members also improved—this merry heart spirit was contagious.

The Bible clearly says in Proverbs 17:22 that "a merry heart does good, like medicine, But a broken spirit dries the bones." We are so happy not to be visiting a valley of dry bones at Shepherd's Arms but rather a refuge where there is joy unspeakable and full of glory. All the little mockingbirds who have been battered, abused, and abandoned now find a new song to sing at Shepherd's Arms. Their song is being transformed from a requiem to a melodic rhapsody—and it's always in a major key.

Chapter 30

IN MY REARVIEW
MIRROR

"Please, show me Your glory."

— EXODUS 33:18

*"So it shall be, while My glory passes by,
that I will put you in the cleft of the rock,
and will cover you with My hand while I
pass by. Then I will take away My hand,
and you shall see My back; but My face
shall not be seen."*

— EXODUS 33:22–23

 My biological mother at age ninety-one had
been chronically ill for six years and two
months. My immediate family and I were her
primary caregivers. The weeks, months, and years
of screaming, moaning, and painful grimaces

etched deeply on her forehead now began to subside and finally transcended into peaceful bliss. What had seemed like an eternity of suffering and persevering in constant pain now transfigured into God's most perfect glory.

The expected finality of physical death came to my mother as I watched, holding her hand and singing hymns of the faith. I knew my singing was different, very special, but I really didn't get it until her final breath was taken and the sigh of peace replaced the anguish that had preceded.

I had stayed up all night with her and had just returned from home in time to personally witness her exodus into heaven. Jesus and my mother waited on me to return before taking flight into glory. I knew Jesus was very close during the singing, but I never knew He was there to personally escort her into glory until I looked back in my spiritual rearview mirror after they left. Then I saw and recognized His glory. All the while Jesus had placed me in the cleft of the Rock and covered me with His hand as He passed by. The peace I experienced was glorious. Then as He removed His hand, I saw Him in my rearview mirror.

Isn't that the way we discover who God is and where He has been? Don't we always recognize Him as we analyze His fingerprints and divine etchings after we think He has gone? Immanuel simply lifts the veil to give us glimpses of His glory. His actions always confirm His Word and His deity.

The truth of the matter is this: We cannot see God, feel God, experience God, or know God unless he chooses to reveal Himself to us. Job knew this, as He said in Job 23:3, 10: "If only I knew where to find Him . . . I would plead my case. . . . Yet He knows the way I have taken; when He has tested me, I will come forth as gold" (BSB). Job knew it wasn't him finding God, but God finding him. God is sovereign, and He rules and reigns in His universe as the Creator and Sustainer of all life.

After my mother's body was pronounced dead by the medical staff, I quickly called my husband and daughter to return to the facility. We sat for a while with my mother's lifeless, cold body and wept for our loss. When the funeral home arrived to pick up my mother's body, Mary Anna and I followed the stretcher outside and watched as they lifted my mother into the black minivan the funeral home was using as a hearse.

My mind was racing with memories of my mama as I viewed the stiff body covered with a blue funeral home blanket. Under that blue blanket was the woman who taught me to tie my shoes, say my prayers, eat my vegetables, and brush my teeth. She was the one whose fingers were broken and arms were cut with glass by a distraught war veteran as she was protecting me. My mama, whose cold body lay on that stretcher, was the one who cooked the delicious gravy and biscuits that my daddy baptized our kitchen walls with. She was the one who quizzed me every day asking if I had had a good bowel movement and if I had done my homework and practiced my piano lessons. She was the lady who taught me to work hard and share what I had earned with the Lord first and then with others. This was the woman who protected me and worked hard to provide for me. Now she was gone from my realm into a higher one.

In my heart I knew Jesus had ordained this moment from eternity past because the Bible clearly tells us in Hebrews 9:27 that "it is appointed for men to die once, but after this the judgment" and Psalm 31:15 tells us that "my times are in Your hand." Psalm 139:16 in the Passion Translation explains it best: "Before I'd ever seen the light of day, the number of days you planned for me were already recorded in your book." My mama passed the baton on to me and now I was the matriarch of the family and the responsibility rested with me.

The day my mama brought me into the world was October 24, 1948, and the day Jesus took her home to heaven was October 22, 2014, just two days shy of my birthday. The very next day after her death I spent the entire day packing up her personal belongings and was totally exhausted physically and emotionally by dusk. Our daughter called me and asked me to please drive by the mission before going home because she wanted to see me. When I pulled into the parking lot of Shepherd's Arms, I caught a glimpse of the most beautiful baby-blue brand-new Volkswagen Bug I had ever seen or thought of seeing. What on earth was going on? When Mary Anna was in medical school, I had driven an old makeshift vehicle or caught a ride with my husband in his truck so we could use our funds to provide a newer model auto for Mary Anna. Now for a surprise birthday gift Mary

Anna had special-ordered me this awesome new car. This was her first large purchase as she began to practice medicine as an ob-gyn physician.

The Lord had strategically scheduled this sweet gift at a time of great sadness and loss to help ease some of the intense pain. I immediately named it "Baby Car." Mary Anna has accused me more than once of worshiping that car and making an idol of it. Actually I loved that car so much I used to take naps in it while it was parked in our driveway. Maybe I did love that car too much but only because it represented such love coming from our daughter. Once again, I could look into my rearview mirror and see the fingerprints of God boldly etched on the side of that car.

So many marvelous memories surfaced as I studied God's fingerprints on my life and remembered sixty-eight years of being the daughter of a strong, amazing woman; thirty-six years of being a mother to a marvelous daughter; thirty-eight years of marriage to the greatest man on earth; and twenty-five years of ministry at Shepherd's Arms Rescue Mission, where it felt as if I had never worked a day in my life. Working with

Jesus in the work He ordains takes the exhaustion and fatigue away.

As I continued to look in my rearview mirror, I saw there was still some very important unfinished business looming in the shadows. My mama never lived to see the completion of the building project at Shepherd's Arms from this side of the universe. Perhaps the view from the balcony is clearer with a more accurate perspective. Fourteen long years we had waited for the Lord to provide resources to complete this building expansion for a much-needed homeless shelter.

Can you imagine driving into the mission parking lot each morning and seeing an empty 10,500-square-foot monolith of bricks and mortar staring back at you, seemingly silently shouting words at you like *failure, rejected, incomplete*? Discouragement was so challenging to ward off. Finally one morning I just drove into the parking lot and began to weep uncontrollably, crying out to God, asking if we had missed Him on this one. Next the words came forth and I said to God, "Okay, God—not my will but Yours be done. Lord, I'm tired, discouraged, fearful, and I need You to help me by strengthening my arms so I can raise them up to praise You once again." I immediately thought of Nehemiah and his prayer in Nehemiah 6:9 saying, "O God, strengthen my hands."

When I looked to the left up to Lookout Mountain from the mission yard, I could see multiple houses for single families that cost much more than this shelter. And as I looked to the right from the front yard of the mission, I could see multiple houses on Missionary Ridge for single families that cost much more than this one shelter for homeless women and children. What were we doing wrong? I began to wonder if at the age of sixty-eight I would live long enough to see this project finished to the glory of God.

Perhaps Noah felt a little peer pressure when he spent one hundred years building the ark. Then there was Solomon, the wisest man around town, who took twenty years to build the temple. The skeptics in Chattanooga had criticized and laughed at us for not borrowing money and completing this project faster. At this point we had already invested over a million dollars in the project and had another $200,000 saved in the bank. Then one day the breakthrough came as my husband and I and our board paid a visit to a very large foundation in Chattanooga requesting the funds to complete the building. We were turned down initially, but the Lord had strategically placed His representatives in that meeting. Later on they contacted us about helping gather the remaining funds to finish the building.

The final funds to complete the building came from the Maclellan Foundation, The McKenzie Foundation, The Robert and Kathrina Maclellan Foundation, the May Family, and Covenant Transport. Hundreds of other faithful partners had given hundreds of thousands of dollars already. This was a combined effort of many of God's children leading to full fruition of this much-needed facility.

The next eighteen months were spent finishing the interior of the building. The Lord provided the most wonderful Christian contractor to oversee the work. When we arrived on the construction site every morning at seven o'clock, we would find our contractor, Mark, on his knees praying, asking God's blessings on the day. Finally, in January 2018 the dedication of Nancy's House at Shepherd's Arms was celebrated. Nancy Maclellan was significantly instrumental in the acquisition of funding for the last phase of the building so the building was named "Nancy's House" in her honor. She helped open the doors of the new shelter for homeless women and children on January 2018, and in May of the same year Jesus Christ opened the doors of His Father's house for Nancy Maclellan, who had fought a very courageous battle with ALS Disease.

Now this fourteen-year project valued at approximately three million dollars was finished, furnished, and dedicated to the Lord Jesus Christ. The first year one hundred fifteen homeless moms and children lived at Nancy's House. Each little mockingbird in residence had been abused and battered in one way or another prior to living at the mission. Now the peace of Jesus settled quickly over each resident. An attitude of gratitude was kindled in every heart and life. The song being emulated from every little fledgling was "To God be the glory, great things He has done."[15]

Here in my home state of Tennessee back in 1933 the mockingbird was chosen to be our state bird.

---

15 Fanny Jane Crosby, "To God Be the Glory."

What a great choice of avian! Did you know that mockingbirds are masterful musicians who can sing up to two hundred songs, including their own original compositions as well as the songs of other birds? They are intense, masterful listeners and mimic and project with precision the sounds they hear around them. Many people symbolize mockingbirds as a picture of innocence that is to be protected and whose voices are to be projected.

My personal view of mockingbirds is one of great respect because I believe mockingbirds are sounding boards of the environment around them. Their voices symbolize the weak among us that need protection from the strong around them. We should be avid listeners to the songs they sing and be mindful to honor and take them to heart. Isn't it true that we are all mockingbirds on one level or another? Our lives reflect the influences of those around us who have shaped us by their words and powerful touch whether it be mother, father, grandmother, grandfather, teacher, preacher, or God Himself.

When I think of the symbolism of mockingbirds, my mind is drawn to our Savior Jesus Christ, who spoke or repeated only those instructions He heard His Father and the Holy Spirit speaking. John 12:49 puts it this way: "For I did not speak on my own initiative, but the Father Himself who sent Me has given Me a commandment as to what to say and what to speak" (NASB). God the Father, Jesus the Son, and God the Holy Spirit were and are personified as the eternal Holy Trinity in perfection representing the perfect community. The imagery of the Creator of all things being slain, beaten, and nailed to a cross echoes the song of His Father's heart of love, mercy, compassion, deliverance, forgiveness, and redemption. His meekness was not weakness but power under control. Jesus Christ, the only begotten Son of the Father, sang in perfect unity and harmony with His Father and the Holy Spirit, saying, "Forgive them, for they know not what they do," as He hung from that cross. Innocent? Yes, perfectly so! Misunderstood? Without a doubt! Abused, battered, and beaten? Gruesomely affirmative! Victorious? Vastly and eternally so!

The bottom line is this: No matter how deep the wounds or intense the pain, or how catastrophic the losses in our lives, the Lord God Almighty can transpose our minor-key requiems and resurrect them into major-key rhapsodies that will heal the brokenhearted and bind up their wounds. The Holy Trinity can set the musical sound waves to the perfect frequency when our melodies are tuned by His divine tuning fork so our ashes of mourning are converted into beauty and our spirit of heaviness is transformed into garments of praise. We need to remember this— please don't kill the mockingbirds who sing around us. Embrace them, respect them, nurture them, protect them, and believe in them. There's always a history nestled deep within their songs that can transform every ounce of pain into the magnificent glory of God.

As I complete this final chapter, I am celebrating my seventy-first birthday. It's been an interesting but totally fruitful journey of transitioning from the early pain of childhood as an innocent little fledgling to the joys of being a more mature and hopefully wiser old bird. All those years of sitting in God's waiting room have really paid marvelous spiritual dividends. We can learn so much just by being still, waiting, and knowing that He is God as we listen closely to the sounds around us as well as those inside us. I have only begun to learn what Isaiah 64:4 really means as it whispers this truth in my spiritual ears: "For since the beginning of the world Men have not heard nor perceived by ear, Nor has the eye seen any God besides You, Who acts for the one who waits for Him." As I look around God's waiting room, it is always filled with baby mockingbirds who are either wounded, struggling, abused, bewildered, or preparing to take flight as they listen and learn to obey God's profound message in Isaiah 40:28–31. Listen very closely to these words of wisdom that begin with two questions:

> *Have you not known? Have you not heard? The everlasting God, the Lord, The Creator of the ends of the earth, Neither faints nor is weary. His understanding is unsearchable. He gives power to the weak, And to those who have no might He increases strength. Even the youths shall faint and be weary, And the young men shall utterly fall, But those who wait on the Lord Shall renew their strength; They shall mount up with wings like eagles, They shall run and not be weary, They shall walk and not faint.*

> — ISAIAH 40:28–31

Please don't kill the mockingbirds around you. Grant them the impeccable gift of ample time in the waiting room of the Ancient of Days. Nurture, encourage, strengthen, and love them until God's healing manifests fully. Then when it is time, instruct them to take flight and soar like eagles for the glory of God. Amen!